The Economies of Queer Inclusion

The Economies of Queer Inclusion

Transnational Organizing for LGBTI Rights in Uganda

By S.M. Rodriguez

LEXINGTON BOOKS
Lanham • Boulder • New York • London

Published by Lexington Books
An imprint of The Rowman & Littlefield Publishing Group, Inc.
4501 Forbes Boulevard, Suite 200, Lanham, Maryland 20706
www.rowman.com

6 Tinworth Street, London SE11 5AL

An earlier version of chapter 1 appears in the journal, *Comparative Sociology*, volume 16, issue 3.

British Library Cataloguing in Publication Information Available

Library of Congress Cataloging-in-Publication Data

Names: Rodriguez, S.M., author.
Title: The economies of queer inclusion : transnational organizing for LGTBI rights in Uganda / S.M. Rodriguez.
Description: Lanham, Maryland : Lexington Books, 2019. | Includes bibliographical references and index.
Identifiers: LCCN 2018048499 (print) | LCCN 2018052769 (ebook) | ISBN 9781498581721 (electronic) | ISBN 9781498581714 (cloth : alk. paper) | ISBN 9781498581738 (pbk. : alk. paper)
Subjects: LCSH: Gay liberation movement--Uganda. | Gay liberation movement--Uganda--International cooperation. | Gay rights--Uganda. | Gays--Legal status, laws, etc.--Uganda. | Gay activists--Uganda.
Classification: LCC HQ76.8.U33 (ebook) | LCC HQ76.8.U33 R63 2019 (print) | DDC 306.76/6096761--dc23
LC record available at https://lccn.loc.gov/2018048499

Contents

Preface

Considering a Methodology of Connection

Aren't you terrified? Don't you fear for your life when you go out there?

A few people, people who love me, sincerely ask this question before, around, and after my trips to Kampala, Uganda. The question is typically followed by an earnest reminder *you're gay. They're persecuting gays.*

At first, I wasn't sure how to handle this interaction. In 2013, shortly before I went to Uganda that June, this question came up again and again: people who cared brought it up (often only one time per person, but since there are a few of them, I felt like I had to answer this every day for the month leading up to my trip).

Each iteration added shape to my response. The asker mattered at first; whether they were white or not, male or female, older or younger, straight or not, etc. Eventually, however, I realized that certain groups of my friends and loved ones didn't ask this at all. That it didn't even occur to them. But before I get into the whom and whys, I'll write my standard answer:

Yes, I am gay. I'm also Black. I'm also read as a woman. I'm also young (often read as a minor). There is not a day in my [then] 25 years that I haven't feared for my life because of my identity.

I grew up Black in white supremacist territory in rural Florida, where the combination of property and gun "rights" trump my right to live. I was born and later returned, a queer woman, to New York City, where violence against and murder of trans and queer women occur regularly. Our anti-black justice system—the law and the enforcers—targets me, my family, my closest friends everyday. Vigilantes target me, my family, my closest friends every day. It never occurred to me to be "extra" afraid about spending time in

Kampala. If anything, I thought perhaps I could finally take my skin off. (This didn't happen, but I anticipated it.)

It is mostly those who haven't had more than one axis of oppression who ask this. And only one axis of oppression is what I consider a privilege. Straight white women, white LGBTQ men, and straight black men astounded me with their concern. My puzzlement, in turn, was always unexpected. We had an unmistakable disconnection. *Didn't you realize my life was in danger when I traveled to your office, favourite restaurant, neighborhood? When the police at Jay Street-Metrotech stopped me as I threw my trash into the waste receptacle?*

With some, particularly with an uncle of mine, I took the time to remind of connection. *Do you fear for your life in this country, as a Black immigrant man? When you walk into your all-white workspace, in the middle of opulent NYC, do you fear anti-black violence and harassment that comes along with being seen as a trespasser?* He remembered and nodded. To be Black in this world is to live with terror, whether you are in the poorest nation or the richest. The option is slow death[1] or a meaningless one, but regardless Black death is largely discounted.

In New York, I fear for my life and bodily integrity when I walk home. When I hear a knock on the door. When cops see me. When people question my gender performativity. In Florida, I fear for my life when I pass by land that has hand-painted "no entry" signs, even when they're public. I fear for my life when I pass the unpaved roads that lead into woods. I fear for my life when the sheriff's deputies follow me. There were many Daniel Holtzclaws before that name meant anything to anyone: white police who abuse black women with impunity, because black women, in particular are framed as not "perfect victims," not credible and in other words, deserving.[2] And these Holtzclaws are scattered throughout this country. They were the boogieman of my youth; lessons about not driving at night, or having a phone on if a police car tails mine on a dark or quiet street.

These experiences inspire my conversation about methodology. I aspired to and eventually practiced what I consider a methodology of connection. This methodology informed the way I approached my participation, observation, and engagement with queer and nonqueer communities in Uganda and New York City. Recognition of this embeddedness was crucial if my aim were to combat what I understood as a fundamental disconnect between Western social analysts, actors, and activists and Ugandan analysts, actors, and activists.

HOW I ENTERED THE RESEARCH

I began my research in 2010, shortly after the October 2009 proposal of the Anti-Homosexuality Bill. As I read the (dreaded) comments sections on article after article, saw exchanges on social media newsfeeds, and engaged in conversations with Americans about the proposed legislation in Uganda, I became more and more agitated by the xenophobia and absence of desire to understand: the disconnection. A truly horrific number of people dismissed the proposal as evidence of a natural, *African homophobia;* a reiteration of the black savagery they had already come to expect. In the same vein of what Amar Wahab terms the "*Jamaicanization* of homophobia" in Canada (2016), there is an active construction of certain racialized groups as the embodiment of homophobia; that it is not the political residue of historical processes of Western colonialism and nation-state building, but an inborn flaw of backwards (Black) peoples. Homophobia is viewed myopically, as a behavior, rather than an institution created by and for nation-states, supported by individual attitudes. When stepping back from the viewpoint, one can see that the anti-gay attitudes espoused in Uganda are neither unique nor new; that although they developed in a particular political moment, the attitudes have more connections than disconnections to other anti-gay mobilizations.

I entered this research with personal understanding and experience with the effects of British colonialism on queer self-determination. These conversations stemmed from before I entered adulthood, as I struggled for familial acceptance, love, support, and guidance in my life (as a young lesbian). By 15, I felt like I had already heard it all: nationalist, religious, and racial anti-gay discourse; discourse that invoked criminality, immorality, and racial self-hatred. The Ugandan sentiments were redundant to me. However, they were brand new to (mostly white) Americans! What was worse than that newness is that those who had the least knowledge and experience had the most power and greatest profile. Predictably, that power was thrown around pre-emptively and long before any situational analysis or contextualized advice we heard *Cut their aid! Sanction them! Arrest the homophobes for incitement to violence!* Every power play that the US could have was debated or threatened in 2010. Accordingly, and perhaps feverishly, I began to collect and note them all.

Another fascinating wave of thought arose as European-Americans questioned the number of queer Africans who could possibly exist. As they deployed the universalizing discourse of homosexuality—that it has existed everywhere, always, and is inborn in select individuals (per the "Born this Way"-Gaga logic), they simultaneously held an exceptionalist logic, that queer and *black* (and specifically *African-born*) must be especially rare.

I began to question the effect of these disjointed, public, American sentiments on the very legislation against which they cried out. *How is this trans-*

national politic inscribed in legislation? I also questioned how American exceptionalism informed the US-based LGBT advocacy that sought to empower or 'protect' Ugandans. *How do American activists, specifically the ones "working on this issue" understand their positionality; their work? How do they imagine themselves as helping?* I then turned to question the movement borne from this interplay. *How does the movement function at the intersection of a disfiguring transnational politic and a harmful nationalist politic?* This book, and the methodologies that I relied upon in order to write it, follow the evolution of these questions and my observations while investigating for answers.

WHAT I MEAN BY METHODOLOGY. . .

I'd like to explain how I use the word "methodology." Although I am a sociologist and this is a sociological work, I am quite inspired by multidisciplinary analyses. For this reason, I do not take for granted even the term "methodology" as do many within sociology. Paola Saukko (2003), for example, explains the following about the term:

> The difference made by the Greek epithet 'logos' (knowledge) is that, whereas methods refer to practical 'tools' to make sense of empirical reality, methodology refers to the wider package of both tools and a philosophical and political commitment that come with a particular research 'approach.'

Methodology encompasses the logic behind both my questions and my methods: it is the motivation of my work. Therefore, this section in which I discuss methodology will not read as strictly a procedural guide. It will foremost guide you to understand the logic that predicated and continued my questioning; that took me to Kampala; and that granted me entry to the precious politics of my participants. It will also explain the forms of research that are privileged within the text.

This book first and foremost employs *counter-storytelling* as a tool that merges qualitative sociology and various ethnographic forms. Counter-storytelling is a critical race methodology developed by Solórzano and Yosso (2002). It counters the deficits in dominant, oppressive narratives so as to put forward new analyses grounded in experiential knowledge. These counter-narratives have an explicit goal of challenging traditional research paradigms that often develop from racist, sexist, or colonialist viewpoints, a well-worn critique of ethnography.

I, at times, tell stories autoethnographically. Autoethnography generates personal reflections as anecdotes that unearth important cultural and interactional themes. These "*I-you-we stories*" (Adams and Jones 2011) stress that through reflexivity one may situate richly textured personal events in larger political processes and structures. Putting forward stories of how various actors interact with me contextualizes the desires, shapes, and motivations of those actors. Although I always stay the same, interpretations of my body change vastly in different spaces and therefore reveal themes of sociological import. Assumptions of my power, wealth, education (or, more often lack thereof) often guided my treatment and access during this research. Autoethnographic notes in the chapters allow me to make note of that difference in access and generate analyses as to its derivation, rather than dismiss what I could not see as inexistent.

I also use interactions, conversations, and observations that developed from interviewing and ethnography. Rather than strictly adhering to and presenting interview data, conversations that occurred during fieldwork play an important role in what I present here. Due to the pressing safety concerns, I never audio-recorded conversations from the field. I instead handwrote notes, with every participant's name, place of interest, and meeting place meticulously coded. These notes would be nearly impossible to decrypt, as any potentially identifying words appeared as amalgams of names, places, and times arranged in an order that I have never shared. Therefore, with regard to the methods of data collection, there were far more precautions and considerations that I tasked myself with in order to do this work ethically. Many qualitative methodologists experience particularized ethical concerns when working with what the Institutional Review Board (IRB) considers *vulnerable populations* (Blee and Currier 2011). Interestingly, kuchu Ugandans fall into this category because they are "people involved in illegal activities" rather than their actual vulnerability for judicial and extrajudicial violence. I intended that, should my notes, laptop or be subpoenaed, kuchus could not be outed.

Another important ethnographic practice that I use developed from a workshop hosted by anthropologists Melissa Forbis and Jeffrey Juris, called "Militant (or Engaged) Ethnography." This convening of scholars helped me understand methodology as this convergence of theory and methods, and to treat it especially carefully. Militant ethnography involves "a politically engaged and collaborative form of participant observation carried out from within rather than outside grassroots movements" intended to "break down the distinction between researcher and activist during the moment of fieldwork" (Juris 2007). It is through this (un)learning that I felt affirmed for having embedded myself within the project, both practically (in terms of the movement) and ontologically (in terms of the systems, the world, etc.). After fighting through the sociological distancing between "researcher" and "subject" (words that I cannot identify with and that make me instinctively recoil), I was introduced to scholar-activist practices uplifting the significance of rooted, activist methodologies.

Methodology of the Oppressed (Sandoval 2000), *Decolonizing Methodologies* (Tuhiwai Smith 1999) and *Racing Research; Researching Race* (Twine and Warren 2000) supported this methodological development as I continually need to recenter antiviolence while navigating academia. The question of *how to do this research in a way that didn't reproduce violence* reemerged, especially as I moved through the fieldwork. The best way that I can do this is to inscribe my anxieties; to treat uncertainty, itself, as an important tool.[3]

As disciplinarily incorrect as this may be, I am not an "expert." I will never be an expert on a struggle that I do not contend with daily. What I would like to accomplish with my analysis is a contribution to our (QPOC/activist-academic) collective understanding of what hurts and what helps our movement (against Western imperialism and for the advancement of queer lives in the Black diaspora); what we need to continue fighting against; what tools we need in order to sustain our battle.

I offer this as one dimension of how to survive. When I say survive, I mean it literally: individually and collectively. Queer and trans people of African descent are organizing, in this very moment, throughout the world in order to create a world where our bodies, beings, and dreams are valued as contributions. We are also attempting to survive the increased threat of sexual assault, rape, and murder. Therefore, while this book focuses on Uganda and the United States, the takeaways are intended for the entire Diaspora. I want our movements to survive for as long as we need to organize for liberation.

The thread of this narrative, hopefully conveyed both in the way I write/see and in the content I provide, is that there are certain connections to which we need to remain true and there are critical disconnections of which we should remain aware. I have not yet read a work that details this, and so, rather than merely a literary or intellectual offering, it is here that I envision my contribution.

MILITANT ETHNOGRAPHY: ENGAGEMENT AND FEELING IN INQUIRY

> *"Compassion hurts. When you feel connected to everything, you also feel responsible for everything. And you cannot turn away. Your destiny is bound with the destinies of others. You must either learn to carry the Universe or be crushed by it. You must grow strong enough to love the world, yet empty enough to sit down at the same table with its worst horrors."* (Boyd 2002)

I hadn't read this quote before I left for Kampala, but I knew the feeling quite well. It led me to revisit a moment that I had in Kampala in 2013. On a day in June, I made an effort to quite literally "sit down at the same table" and engage in a conversation that could only be described as both horrible and great: I went out with a group of college students that clustered around 18 years old.

The hostess of my bed and breakfast had a nephew, Daniel, who was kind, sociable, and pretty funny. She told me that he was good looking and that I would like him. He was much younger than me, but had charisma. I had to laugh at this situation, as I had only been there a week at that point and had been set up to meet someone's cousin/nephew/brother several times. I hadn't yet shared my orientation with anyone, so it was an expected accompaniment to the territory.

I got a good sense of his character, through conversation and hanging out at the bed and breakfast a few times. We had a mutual understanding by then (that I wasn't, and would never be interested in him; that we could test each other's politics without any personal fallout). He talked about his polygynous politic, thinking that it would provoke or stir me. I shared my positions on polyamory and provoked him with the concept of a woman with many lovers. We laughed at our disagreements.

After we established this rapport (which didn't take long; he is honestly quite charismatic), he invited me to venture off property with him. We met up with several of his friends from Makerere at a local tiki bar called Fuego in Muyenga. They were engineering and medical students, a familiar-feeling, nerdy crowd of teens. Over beers they chatted about school, their anxiety about finals, and my hopes to connect with "feminist organizers" in Kampala.

After a second round of beers, Daniel came over to me and nudged, *"why don't you talk about what you're really interested in, feminist."* I laughed and whispered, *"how do you think they'll respond?"* He responded along the lines of he hadn't ever broached the subject, but he's interested in what they'd say. I sat pensively, flirting with the idea of a roundtable discussion about homosexuality with this group. Then, Daniel interrupted my deliberation with, *"Guys, she wants to know what you think about the government's current homosexual obsession."* Not quite how I'd phrase it, but fun enough.

The conversation sparked, excitedly.

> *"I don't want gays to die!"*
> *"I, personally, don't care if they die but I don't want to be responsible for their deaths."*
> *"I don't want a bigger government! They already try to have so much control over us!"*
> *"What kind of freak would I be to care what these people do in their own bedrooms?"*
> *"Yeah, if they consent and want to have fun let them."*
> *"With all the women who are raped? With all the children abused? Why should we care what people do when they don't hurt each other and want to be*

> *together?"* replied a girl who Daniel was dating and who had a lot of interest in women's movements and groups.

Agitated, however, became Semi, a small guy with a big presence. He interjected *"Well, I personally would kill all gays."* The group, mostly shocked, reminded him that he had just said, in another context, that people should have the right to life and freedom. One student responded incredulously, *"are you kidding me? Look at our poverty and starvation, why would you waste the time?!"* Semi continued with the abuse that he had heard gays were committing on children throughout the country. Smugly, he finished with confidence that he could fix both national problems.

I sat next to one 18-year-old engineering student with large glasses on; he had a sweet smile and a shy chuckle and reminded me of a baby cousin I hadn't seen in years. He leaned in, amidst the discussion, and whispered a question with a newfound interest. His shy smile turning slightly suggestive he asked, *"so, have you ever kissed another woman?"* I laughed without responding, giving a subtle wink and jousted *"the real question is have you?"* But wouldn't he have liked to know. . . I thought.

Curious teenagers; budding political passions; fear, anger, interest, and new realizations of one's citizenship: this is connection. I remembered being 13 and having a conversation on a pool deck with an older, Bajan teenager and my 14-year-old, Jamaican brother about whether or not homosexuality was natural or okay. I remembered the decade of conversations that I had had since then, with people in the diaspora, about what they would/could/should do in response to homosexuality. I remembered Brooklyn; I remembered my Caribbean family. And *I heard them all* in these responses, whether they advocated for acceptance, compassion, turning a blind eye, "correction," or even annihilation.

Connection allowed me to receive these responses with strong love and that wide spaciousness that Boyd referred to in the opening quotation. Connection is what I firmly believe both a movement and a political analysis needs. My people (the people of the African Diaspora) are going through it; figuring out how to love themselves and each other after generations of being convinced they were unworthy of love or compassion. And the way they are figuring this out is through a very different (but always related/sometimes reactive) path than what the colonizers currently take. This is the lens through which I began my work on homophobic nationalism and is detailed in chapter 1.

THE ROLE OF SHIFTING (AS A METHOD) IN CONNECTION (AS A LOGIC)

> *Because nonwhite women have long been multiply oppressed, as part of their political coming-to-consciousness they have had to learn to highlight (or obscure) different aspects of themselves to be able to work effectively within political organizations. . . U.S. third world feminists have become practiced at shifting their ideologies and identities in response to different configurations of power.* (Moya 2002)

> *The differential mode of consciousness functions like the clutch of an automobile, the mechanism that permits the driver to select, engage, and disengage gears in a system for the transmission of power.*(Sandoval 2000)

Differential consciousness requires that we constantly reform our ties—often instantly, but always consciously—in order to create the coalitions and connections necessary for social change. Gloria Anzaldúa (2013), Charisse Jones and Kumea Shorter-Gooden (2004) have all referred to a dimension of this as *shifting*. I will also use shifting, along Moya's thought. Shifting, in her understanding, is the practice that results from U.S. Third World Feminists' experience navigating the power structures reified by the U.S.

This mode of experiencing the world, and the lessons that are gained by it, have important implications that we can use to build analyses. I imagine shifting as a tool in my ethnographic work. It allows me access to various spaces, for a similar purpose: I highlight and use the language of "the academy" in order to get interviews with American transnational workers of Chapter 3 (who specifically valued PhD-level work). On the other hand, I necessarily avoid this language in most other sites. I found that, Matt for example (Chapter 3), was excited to engage with the sociological theory he had learned in his undergraduate career; whereas, in my exclusively-POC organization, academic language is actually referenced explicitly as a violation of our ground rules during meetings. It is considered "outside" language: harmful and exclusive. However, in both meetings, the end goal is the same. We want to get to the possibilities and limits of queer justice work.

Shifting is also self-preservation work. A differential mode of consciousness, like the clutch metaphor that Sandoval uses, is the only way to move forward sustainably. If I did not shift when meeting with the youth at Fuego, I would have been reduced to a stagnant defensiveness. This is to say, that as a U.S. Third World Feminist, or queer person of the African Diaspora, I have the capacity to connect to various lines of thought; I have experienced a particular convergence of politics that allow me to connect to this work. However, without shifting, I would have forgotten the connection that I had to Semi—injuring the project.

At the Militant/Engaged Ethnography Workshop earlier referenced, the facilitators prompted us to complete a five-minute thinking exercise. We were to quickly reflect and write the "Scene of the Crime"—our entry point into the analysis we hoped to build. I'll share it here, in hopes that it may provide a useful illumination:

> *I came out as a lesbian almost as soon as I grabbed an understanding of the word. It's not that I didn't have SGL or GNC family members, it's that the L word was new and unfamiliar. Between 14 and 15 I told my parents—immigrant parents both with lived histories of British colonialism—that I identified with this word, this imagined identity, category, and community that I had heard about on TV. For this, I was thrown prematurely into a circumstance where I needed to provide for myself—in terms of material and emotional needs. I became a youth activist at 18 years old, after gaining a sense of agency and self-worth. I embedded myself in a "LGBTQ rights" organization and learned and shared a political education that was handed down to me about the civil rights that I should believe in: monogamous unions, worker's rights, aiding the project of militarization. I regurgitated these beliefs and by the time I was 20, shared them with hundreds of other students.*
>
> *When I graduated, I left the façade of college privilege. After experiencing and witnessing the devastation of poverty I scratched out those ideas, questioning how my struggle ever became that in the first place. My brown skinned, SGL and GNC people were being stabbed, hosed down in the temporary homes they squatted in, raped and robbed by customers. I toned down the PE (political education) and instead listened and watched; I realized a position truer to me.*
>
> *I now study the ways in which a movement with a recent history of British colonialism and currently situated in purposeful, world systems poverty navigates the transnational hostility of LGBT imperialism (homonationalism) and domestic (anti-homosexual) hostility. Accordingly, I figure in the anti-blackness of homonationalism and the anti-Westernness of homophobic nationalism. I see myself as embedded in each facet of the Ugandan movement, although not necessarily a part of the Ugandan movement.*

Over half of the roughly 76 countries that currently criminalize sodomy do so as a result of British colonial law.[4] Thirty-four of these countries are in Africa; 10 are in the Americas. In this way, the movement that I study is my own. It is the same movement that I build for in the US; the same movement that my Jamaican and Trinidadian kin build for in the West Indies. Our destinies are bound, connected. Therefore, this is the logic to the various qualitative methods that I chose and the impetus to my analytical work in this Ugandan case. I chose to focus on Uganda, rather than a closer country (in regard to geography or kinship) because it was evident that the proposal of the Anti-Homosexuality Bill provided a critical, historical moment through which the politics of transnational organizing could be very clearly viewed. I anticipated that the moment would not last long, as both 'the media' and the international human rights regime are critiqued as having short attention spans.

CONCERNS AND UNCERTAINTIES: ANALYTICAL DISCONNECTIONS

In the ending sentence of my "Scene of the Crime" practice, I stated that I am "not necessarily a part" of the movement. The statement serves as recognition that this is a different iteration, grouping, and manifestation of queer justice building. Although I am embedded in queer movements more generally, I would do this work a disservice not to detail my own points of disconnection from the specific movement in Kampala.

Ironically, a brief exchange on *Hannibal*, a television series on at the time of my research, quite poetically introduces this connection-disconnection conflict. Hannibal's family's maid, Chiyoh, listens to Hannibal's eternal lover/mortal enemy, Will, as he quietly states:

> *"Birds eat thousands of snails every day.*
> *Some of those snails survive digestion*
> *and emerge to find*
> *they've traveled the world*
> *in the belly of the beast."*

In my melancholy moments, particularly as I walked from Muyenga to Kibuli toward and then over the train tracks, I thought about how I got there. To contend with one's status as a survivor is always a conflicting confession of both privilege and loss. Snail or otherwise, I reflected on what I may be bringing or perpetuating, by traveling there. I was acutely aware, at all times, that I had been digested and granted travel by an American institution. This constant awareness made me center and reaffirm my accountability. *I am here for the movement; I am here for my people. I am not here for a literary contribution, to be inevitably locked in the ivory tower. I am not here for an American university. I am capable of staying true to my agency, my values, this action.* Affirmations and reminders by scholars such as Shanti Parikh (2004) are invaluable: "black feminists, third wave feminist scholars have an obligation to our ancestors, disciplines, communities and ourselves to strengthen alliances and refine theoretical frameworks and tools of inquiry (p. 87). However, the conflict—the question of how to do this—persisted and often stifled me.

I, the snail, have never been free. My agency is mediated by my (ultimately imperialist) affiliations: my passport, my institution, the money I'd been granted. It felt all-consuming at times. I had this overwhelming awareness that my survival was a fluke and that all that I saw was all that the bird had allowed me to see.

Of course, there was also the consideration that the belly in which I reside had a positive effect on my analysis. It, in many ways, allows me to see the inner workings of imperialism so clearly. Black Americans and Black immigrants in America have particularized and precious insight into US justice, educational, and economic systems. We understand who benefits and how; we understand systematic exclusion. In an unpublished manuscript, in 1985, Aida Hurtado says we "are more like urban guerrillas trained through everyday battle with the state apparatus" (via Sandoval 1991). Couple that with the textbook and community learning that I have sought out and I can affirm that my insight is valuable.

However, there were moments when disconnection overwhelmed me; when my confidence in my analytic and politic faltered. These moments largely stemmed from unanticipated conversations about race (*what are you?* you're not black here! maybe red. . .?); my incoherent performance of femininity (you are so masculine! why are you so comfortable around the men? you look so pretty, I don't understand why you have these dreadlocks); and assumptions about whether or not I had money like "the whites."

Moments like this appear anecdotally in this work, my interaction with Kai in Chapter 4 is one such example, when they ask "*why is she here?*" Another similar instance occurred as I interacted with Michael. Michael was from what more prominent activists call a "briefcase organization" (that I will discuss a bit further in Chapter 4) that I had met with in 2013. I sustained a relationship with him for months after, until he shut down his organizational affair in December.

By January, Michael sent me a message requesting money—$82 by tomorrow. The request rang similarly to Peter's (also introduced in Chapter 4), who asked for $100 on 10/31 for November rent; who continued to ask for financial support. This financial disconnect ensured that I maintained awareness of my national/economic privilege, but simultaneously aware of my limited ability to be actually helpful. Yes, I could afford to pay Ugandan rent on my American salary; but I couldn't afford to pay my American rent *and* support anyone financially. I lived paycheck to paycheck at the time, experiencing inflated New York rent (where a bedroom in a shared apartment ran at least $800 a month) that ate the actual majority of my university paycheck (roughly $1,400/month before tax).

However, beyond not "being able" to help, I debated whether or not I would if I could. I remembered that whole wave of "sponsoring African children" that hit the US in the 90s. The idea itself, of financially helping those in need, never disturbed me, but I did have a substantial critique of the exploitative methods of organizations that set up these networks. I was, admittedly, too young to really experience it during the phase. This situation set up huge, conflicting political questions for me. Jamaicans in the States very commonly experience similar requests. In search for some connection to guide my answers, I remembered distant family members or community members from my mother's rural hometown asking for money consistently. It was very common for my mom to distribute clothing, shoes, toys, electronics when she (or we) went back. However, I couldn't remember for how long she had sent remittances. Had she? How did she feel about it? Uganda clearly isn't "my home country," but at the same time, I've never felt like I had a home country (or a nationality, beyond what my passport technically says). It felt just as much "home" as Jamaica had, or Trinidad, and much more than the rural town in Florida where I actually spent most of my childhood. Being "first generation" meant that these answers felt rather vague and unformed. They became a consistent source of anxiety.

I didn't, and couldn't, honestly question Michael or Peter's need. Community members who figured their organization out had just threatened Michael and his partners. However, as opposed to Peter, he was more of an adult and had entrepreneurial experience. He could bounce back. Peter, on the other hand, was 18 and dealing with depression and a very low chance of finding "real" employment (due to his inexperience and lack of education). And although I could buy food and pay for his transportation when we met up and give him change while I was in Kampala—I simply couldn't finance his life from the States.

This, however, caused Peter to grow very disenchanted with me and sever our relationship. His final request came around the time Michael sent his in January. He stopped talking to me until he heard I was back in Kampala in May, saying that he had been angry.

This, which I understand as a major disconnection, caused me to reconsider our transnational "friendship" and camaraderie. It also made me question if my only value to people I had made relationships with in Kampala was in my perceived money and willingness to share or redistribute it. Both Michael and Peter unfriended me after I had said I didn't have any money to send. What was my perceived usefulness? Limitations? Did people only understand me in terms of "worth"? If so, was I worthwhile?

My hesitance also caused me to question my own values, as redistribution of financial resources is exactly what I believe in. What did I have to give? Why did I believe in my own usefulness?

Ultimately, these self-explorations caused me to question sustainability and what role that has in transnational relationships altogether. They guided my interactions and observations throughout the rest of my analytical pursuit. My answer to that final question, of my own usefulness, became the inspiration for the concluding chapter, on the potentials of Diaspora-centered organizing. Alternatively, my answers to the true value of financial donations are persistently (even if still incompletely) explored throughout the second section of this book.

It is in this way that even the lack of connection played a role in my methodology. When I put connection at the forefront of my mind during this work, I can not only acknowledge the severe disconnections, but also interrogate them; formulate a better project because of them.

The final note of disconnection that I preface this book with is that of the identity "researcher" and my identities as scholar-activist, analyst, and person of African descent. I have to note that historically, my people, my family which is scattered throughout the African diaspora, have had intrusive and parasitic relationships with those who self-define as "researchers," only to experience infantile analyses of blackness and black sexuality. This has occurred largely when "the white gaze" perches in Africa, the Caribbean, and in Black minority communities. We must challenge the notion that research of liberation movements is in its essence a liberatory project: it is not. One must be aware of the "ways in which the pursuit of knowledge is deeply embedded in the multiple layers of imperial and colonial practices" (Tuhiwai Smith, p. 1) and use "humility and honesty" (Parikh 2004, p. 87) to assert and challenge the motivations and methodologies involved.

In pursuit of a transformative project, I connect with anti-imperial, feminist thinkers and organizers. I align my work with the epistemological tradition that upholds self-determination. Therefore, in direct defiance of objectivity, self-determination of SGL and GNC communities of the African diaspora became my research agenda.

> Self-determination in a research agenda becomes something more than a political goal. It becomes a goal of social justice, which is expressed through and across a wide range of psychological, social, cultural and economic terrains. It necessarily involves the processes of transformation, of decolonization, of healing and of mobilization as peoples. The processes, approaches and methodologies—while dynamic and open to different influences and possibilities—are critical elements of a strategic research agenda.
> (Tuhiwai Smith 1999, p. 116)

Black peoples, in Africa and throughout the Diaspora, need to decolonize the politics of the GRIM, *gay rights international movement*! In order to conceptualize a project that advances self-determination for SGL and GNC communities, we must engage strategically with our methods and with our language. It is with these considerations that I begin this book.

NOTES

1. *Slow death* refers to the physical wearing out of the population through capitalist, structural subordination and governmentality (Berlant 2007).
2. In 2015, Oklahoma City police officer Daniel Holtzclaw was found guilty of five counts of rape and 13 counts of sexual assault—all against black women. The Cato Institute found

sexual misconduct to be the second most commonly reported police violation, behind excessive force: 618 police officers were reported in 2010.

3. The idea of treating uncertainty with care is borne from the valuable advice that I received from Melissa Forbis and Jeffrey Juris.

4. Sao Tome and Principe, Lesotho, and Mozambique all dropped from this list in the course of writing this manuscript!

Acknowledgments

I would like to thank Hofstra University and the National Center for Suburban Studies for the LGBTIAQQ Research Initiative Award that supported the final efforts of this work. For the earliest stages of research, I recognize the W. Burghardt Turner Fellowship at Stony Brook University, the Center for Inclusive Education, and the American Sociological Association's Minority Fellowship Program for research and conference travel support and precious fellowship communities. Thank you to the blind reviewer of the manuscript, whose incisive comments drastically improved this text. An earlier version of chapter 1 appears in the journal, *Comparative Sociology* (2017) volume 16, issue 3, pages 393–421.

I'd like to extend my sincere gratitude to Michael Schwartz, who has tirelessly elevated my scholarship and understanding of social movements and social structure. Additionally, a truly wonderful group has supported my writing and theorizing, by reading drafts, attending talks, and providing critical feedback: Cliff Leek, Kathleen Fallon, Jalise R. Burt, Ashley Currier, Godiva Akullo, and Jasmin Young. An even more extensive network provided emotional support during the seven-year journey of this research. Among this network, I'd like to especially acknowledge my parents Lindsay and Sherley; siblings, Damian, Ayesha, and Cyprian; and wife, Athena Belle-Fairplay, whose artistry and politics continually inspire me.

Introduction

QUEER ORGANIZING FOR FULL CITIZENSHIP

Mama[1] and her daughter sat next to me on the second and third legs of my flight from New York City to Entebbe, Uganda. Their trip began in London, but the flights connected in Amsterdam. Our massive plane featured 10-seat rows and was nearly full, dropping off and picking up passengers in Rwanda before we all unloaded in Entebbe. Mama, her daughter, and I were, however, some of only a handful of people of African descent on the flight. I couldn't help but notice that all around us were groups of white, European and American young people, many of whom had matching t-shirts or windbreakers.

They were in groups of roughly ten 18-year-olds with one to three accompanying adults. At the gate in Amsterdam and at the stop in Kigali, where we were not allowed off of the plane unless it were our final destination, they stretched their legs, chatted, or formed hand-holding circles. *They prayed.* A number of them got off the plane in Kigali, but twenty minutes later were replaced by similar groups of passengers, loading on to the Entebbe-bound plane from the Rwandan airport.

The sight of youth prayer groups was a familiar one: having grown up in a highly religious, Southern town, I remembered the devout teenagers and their Christian conviction. I thought of one classmate in particular, who had become a missionary. She moved to central Africa while I attended university. Queer, African analyses have shed a stunning light on this topic, especially those that focus on Uganda. The increasing religiosity of the region (Bompani 2016); the presence and effect of foreign Evangelicals on anti-gay perspectives, practices, and law (Kaoma 2009, Ward 2013) and the current process of "re-membering" Christian devotion of pre-colonial Uganda (Rao 2015) have been documented and analyzed with fervor in the new millenium. This new context stunned me, though. I had not anticipated the visual significance of their numbers—even though, of course, I knew the qualitative significance of their continued presence in the region.

Mama, noticing that I was flying alone, struck up casual conversation. She and her daughter were wearing hijabs and had noticeably different accents from one another. As I had hoped, Mama was born and raised in Uganda; her daughter is from London, where they live now. They asked general questions: Where am I heading? Do I have family in Kampala? She was concerned about how I would get around while in Kampala and offered me several phone numbers, remarking that her family has multiple cars.

I made a promise to call them when I had bought a phone and to visit their family home when I've settled in. When I called, several days later, she informed me that she would send her nephew Hassan to retrieve me. We became friends quickly. Soon, I grew close with the entire family, which I found incredibly warm and generous; me, they often remarked they found "so nice" and "different."

One day, well after meeting and growing accustomed to each other, Hassan and I walked through Kansanga. I was heading to the guesthouse in which I had been staying for the summer and he agreed to show me a (curiously long) shortcut. The area is not exceptional, relative to some Kampala neighborhoods that are perhaps atop one of the many hills or nearer to Lake Victoria. So when I saw a building with an architectural particularity, it caught my attention. It was multistory, strikingly white, with beautiful exterior moulding, and looked very out of place. Hassan noticed me noticing it.

"That is where the gays go," he abruptly offered, unsolicited. Having successfully caught me off guard, as he so often enjoys doing, I asked what he meant.

"I mean that is a nightclub and gays party there. . . at the top." He nodded in its direction. Not completely believing him, as he is a straight, Muslim-practicing, cisgender[2] guy who often pulls my leg, I asked, "how do you know that? It looks like a place for rich people."

"Everyone knows this. All gays are rich."
"All gays are not rich, Hassan. Why would you say that?"
"Gays *are* all rich," he laughs, knowingly. "Whites come and pay them like prostitutes."

I probed Hassan a bit, but not too much after this. In the brief conversation that unfolded, Hassan shared with me that "whites" pay Ugandans to be or to say that they are gay and share money for the identity to popularize. As a result, Ugandans who say that they are gay have a particular opportunity to get European/American money, and therefore are rich enough to colonize expensive nightclubs.

Most of Hassan's political opinions provided the foundation for our quickly forming friendship. He wasn't just kind, like his family; he was sharp-witted, brutally honest, bold and politically angry (in a way that reminded me of myself and of *home*). His politics, even those related to sexuality, were largely nuanced. So when he relied on this dogma for homosexuality, the moment struck me; I made note of it. He neither enlisted a religious claim, nor a trope about the harmful health implications of sodomy. Instead, he argued here that *racial outsiders fund it.* I cannot help but conclude that it must, in his eyes, be therefore rooted primarily in racio-economic inequality.

Instead of brushing this off as "untrue" because my experience with this identity is so different, I choose to keep it in mind and to honor his understanding. I don't do this by accepting or agreeing with it, but by thinking it through; giving merit to its formation and its implications. And I will do so throughout this book with a deep questioning of association and identity.

My identity vacillates between the terms *lesbian* and *queer,* the former specifies my desire, the latter accounts for my non-binary gender identity. I was very young when I began to identify as a lesbian, and my note here is merely to state that in my experience, assuming these labels initially had no apparent connection to money or race. Upon the last four years of reflection, since this interaction with Hassan and with this research, I acknowledge that the media that I consumed that taught me of the identity terms (most notably, "The L Word") were both a product of white economic power and white lesbian culture. Nevertheless, my experience countered his imagining of a simple economic exchange between a previously straight person and a "rich" gay person.

More importantly, *kuchu* (LGBTQIA) Ugandans also do not attribute their identity-formation to these economic relationships. An interlocutor tells Stella Nyanzi (2013, p. 960):

> Often new members join us a long time after they started having desires and attractions towards people of the same sex. Most are like this from a young age which can be many years before meeting white people. So, we can be Africans who are homosexual without knowing any white person to teach us about homosexuality.

Regardless of whether or not economic exchanges play a role in romantic or sexual relationships (as they often do, despite geography), they do not lead to identity adoption.

Kuchu, in fact, is a "localized label" (Nyanzi 2013) denoting the status of being a sexual minority and/or gender nonconforming person. It is commonly used in Kampala and encapsulates all LGBTIA labels and identities, including the variations and terms that do not exist outside of Uganda, such as "311 gay" (Minor 2014) or "chapati" (Nyanzi 2013). Analysts using interviewing or (auto)ethnography have generally found that those in Uganda also appropriate various "Western"-derived terms, such as homosexual, gay/lesbian, and circulate the labels as much (or even more) frequently as *kuchu.* Importantly, Nyanzi (2013, p. 959) found that some gay Ugandan men actually reject the *kuchu* identity, citing that it is explicitly sexual and political in ways they found offensive. As the term propagated through a set of Kampala-based activists in the early 2000s (Minor 2014), some Ugandans associate it with a particular, political form.

However, Hassan is—*by far*—not the only person to believe that gay-identity adoption results from sexual patronizing. It is interesting, because we had parallel discussions of the heterosexual, sexual patronizing that occurs between young women and older men. However, in those discussions there is no question of the other-sex sexual desire being *produced* by such arrangements, even if the young person was a virgin beforehand. The tension in Hassan's remarks is obviously a phenomenological one: how has this identity come to exist in Uganda? Is it an event, a temporality, resulting from structural inequality? How do whites support homosexuality and by what motivation?

I inscribe this tension in each chapter of this book. Although I am not interested in the process of identity-assumption, I am interested in the internationalized political economy of homosexuality. These sexual politics, as related to international intervention and development, have created a newfound struggle for international and local actors seeking sexual justice in African cities. The question that initially guided this research was how does sexual justice organizing in Uganda work, when it must contend with domestic and international political processes that are, in and of themselves, conflicting. However, the ethnographic data took me through and beyond social movement strategies, and into a look at the new economies that have formed as a result of international interest in bolstering gay rights efforts. The more pointed question, then, becomes *how does the international political economy of homosexuality form or deform possibilities for queer sexual justice in Uganda?*

I use the theoretical frameworks "homophobic nationalism" and "homonationalism" in order to explore these thoughts in a way that situates the current politic in a historical and global interface. Homophobic nationalism is the impetus of Hassan's comments: it is a complex assemblage of racial and economic tensions reinforced by historical memories of imperialism and anxieties about the nation's current status within the world system.[3] Homonationalism, or *homonormative nationalism,* is a concept originally developed by Jasbir Puar, that aids the understanding of how Core nations use sexual politics for a continued domination over the Periphery. It is a particular "gay rights" politic that reconstitutes a nation's strength by integrating a certain set of homosexuals into its economic, political, and military powers.

Homophobic nationalism describes the particular anti-gay trajectory that Uganda began almost three decades after gaining independence in 1962. Due to the relative youth of the country, Uganda's nationalism must account for "the transnational" in a way that is very different than its Western counterparts, many of which had a nation-state model begin at least centuries earlier and embraced colonization and slavery to amass the wealth required for autonomy. This analysis captures the differences that form when the national project of sexual repression begins in a later, more technologically advanced and more globalized structure of governance, due to a peripheral nation's relationship to structural adjustment and foreign aid.

Homophobic nationalism, in this way, will explain the tendency of impoverished, recently decolonized states to respond to globalized identities such as lesbian, gay, bisexual, transgender, etc. with the hostility generally reserved for imperialist projects. Altogether, combing through the literature that connects sexual citizenship, the World System, and transnational social movements allows recognition of how homophobia, as a national project, proxies as anti-imperialism. It also provides a basis from which we can understand how Western homonationalism counterproductively strengthens homophobic nationalism. Without witnessing Western homonationalism, Hassan and many others would likely not jump to conclusions about sexual minority identities being founded and funded by Western agents.

FROM SEXUAL CITIZENSHIP TO HOMONATIONALISM

Modernity featured nation-states that offer rights and regulations to citizens through a binary, sexed system. The genitalia of human bodies were (and continue to be) ascribed significant meaning, becoming the predominant signifier of character, personality, worth and behavior for humans. People were designated permanent roles; their behavior assignments and social relations inflexibly shaped based off of a simple measurement of external sex characteristics at birth. At adulthood, the actions of those assigned male were subject to the government's regulation; those assigned female were to be regulated by males. The gender, *man*, was understood as the predominant actor in the public sphere, the sector of life that involves the state and society. Those gendered *woman* were relegated to the private sphere, or the sector of life that was meant to exist outside of the realm of the state, government, and view of the public. Although this configuration offered women relative autonomy from the state, it denoted that women's needs, sense of belonging, and transgressions were ultimately a man's responsibility to oversee (de Beauvoir 1949; Millett 1970). This basic framework recognizes that citizenship—or access to the full protections and participation in matters of the state—is sexed (Cossman 2007; Evans 1993; Lister 1990, 1996, 1997).

The nation-state model began in what is called the West, which is now less of a geographic reference than a racial one. The concept of the state intended for (white) men to be the wage laborers, taxpayers, property protectors, and the flag bearers in times of crisis and war. Those designated female began *as* property and now, due largely to global women empowerment movements, constitute various hybrid positions, dependent on the respective nation-state (Tripp 2001a). Women work, consume, and vote with a modicum of protections to ensure access to these dimensions of citizenship, but are still overburdened with and assumed the roles and responsibilities of the private sphere—to the detriment of full participatory parity (Pateman 1988, 1989; Tripp 2001a and b). Therefore, although women may gain access to aspects of citizenship, the constitution of citizenship condemns women to a lesser position.

Importantly, this perspective centering sexual citizenship has provided a theoretical foundation from which critiques have developed. While scholars of sexual citizenship centralized this particular binary, several other, more complex frameworks emerged. Sexual orientation, racial and ethnic identification, and other divisions complicate the notion of primacy of sex and gender subordination within state borders. I will outline, in the following sections, a decades-long trajectory of feminist, womanist, and queer theory, that have brought us to more nuanced understandings of the conflict and oppressions that structure contemporary societies.

Many critical African studies scholars, queer theorists, and Queer African studies scholars regard the gender binary as an invention. Oyēwùmí (1997) stands out as a particularly striking critic of adopting the lens of the gender binary to explain or understand social relations and divisions. Oyēwùmí's central criticism is that the importance of gender divisions cannot and should not be universalized, as constituent institutions such as the nuclear family are peripheral to many African experiences. She uses Nigerian examples, noting that the Yoruba language itself, unlike many Western languages, does not rely on gender as a structuring marker, instead favoring categories that denote age or seniority. As the gender binary relates to Uganda, Nannyonga-Tamusuza's (2002, 2009) historical review of pre-colonial gender in Buganda demonstrates the vast differences between the fixed, Western concepts of man and woman, and such categories in Buganda. Although gender was the marker that structured society, it was situational, fluid, and second to hierarchical status (royalty or commoner):

> The historical construction of gender is dependent on whether one belongs to royalty or the commoners' class. The gender socialization within the palace assigns both the princes and princesses a man gender, and the commoners—both male and female—a woman gender. However the woman gender as-

signed to the commoner males is only situational. They retain a man gender outside the palace contexts (p. 144).

Therefore, while speaking contemporarily of gender and sex in African nations, it is important to ground one's perspective to respect and acknowledge *hybridity,* or the manifestation of new and different political forms that emerge when elements of one society are combined with features of another. This hybridity should guide analyses away from simple dichotomies of oppressed and oppressor, or powerful and powerless. For example, honoring political difference, one could note that the East African Community[4] features the second highest regional rate of women's political representation (36.3 percent), second only to Nordic Europe (42.2 percent).[5] This statistic reaffirms my earlier point that while women may gain access to aspects of citizenship, the constitution of citizenship condemns women to a form of marginality, which holds true in hybridized (African) and centralized (European) national experiences. A rare exception to this lack of parity can be found in Rwanda, where the majority of the parliamentary positions are held by women, largely attributed to the genocide and mass emigration that occurred in 1994.

In addition to and as a crucial component of gender, the nation-state also assigns the citizen a sexual orientation. In this regard, one may recognize the intended and embraced subject of the state as heterosexual. Multidisciplinary and multinational works have produced a grounded understanding of the ways in which the state disables homosexual citizenship (Alexander 1994; Bell 1995; Bell and Binnie 2000; Canaday 2003, 2009; Evans 1993; Richardson 1998; Seidman 2001). This includes how nations have diffused legislative practices of targeting homosexuality and gender nonconformity for exclusion from the real and imagined citizenry (Alexander 1994; Canaday 2003; Luibheid 1998). This also includes how even the fact of birth in a territory does not automatically include a person in the imagined citizenry: health services, employment, and service to the state have been denied to those identified outside of heterosexuality. This exclusion rests largely on reproductive futurist arguments: citizenship relies on erotic and romantic narratives of reproduction (Richardson and Turner 2001). The reproductive citizen is able to reproduce not only generations of future citizens, but through that process, able to reproduce norms and mores of how to relate to the state. This heterosexism renders lesbian and gay people "other" than citizen. They are granted partial citizenship, due to the inability to legally marry, serve in the military, enter the workplace, or adopt children. Therefore, this approach to sexual citizenship centers the role of the state in suppressing queer participation in reproducing the state. Although this politic has played a crucial role in the constitution of the nation-state, it is only one nationalist construction relating to homosexuality; one which we have, both for better and worse, witnessed pivotal transformations in many nations within the early 21st century.

Focusing an analysis on sexual citizenship in Uganda inherently limits the conversation to a particular type of investigation. Tushabe wa Tushabe notes that "LGBTQ identitarian–private relations" are defined within "the state-citizenship machinery of surveillance" as "privacy is understood in postcolonial relations to be between the state and citizens" (p. 18–83). To look at those who hold LGBTI identities in Uganda is to look at the antagonistic relationship between sexuality and the state; not to explore the full ways in which same-gender love, affection or sex exist in Uganda. Indeed, many of those who exchange "same-sex erotic energies" within Uganda have no desire to adopt globalized identities, or any identity around their sexuality. An interlocutor in her study says:

> As nyokwento (maternal aunt) and mother to my children, I know what to do, I know who I am and to whom. Under this roof, Ayebale and I share love, and we are love to one another. These two women are my bitakuri (sweet potatoes), and I am their kitakuri (sweet potato). We deeply care for one another and our families (extended families). What would I be if I became a lesbian? (p. 178–179)

Therefore, various positionalities may structure one's identities, behaviors, and sense of self. This sense of self is always relational, forming in community and in family. To adopt an LGBTI identity would be to radically reshape one's personhood, and to largely be left to seek new communities, with which one may take up new actions, relationships and goals. In Uganda, this may mean the LGBTI identity in its essence requires an increasingly interactive position to the state. One would begin to understand oneself as a citizen, rather than *kitakuri,* as this participant affectionately uses. Importantly, it is also possible that such a shift may indeed *queer* reproductive roles, kinship configurations, and taken-for-granted gender identities such as *woman* in various settings.

Coloring Citizenry: Racialized Sexual Politics around the World

Whereas the foundational assumptions of sexual citizenship imagine a sexed dichotomy as the primary dynamic of separation in nationhood, scholars of color critiqued this early perspective meticulously in order to complicate the early understandings. *Intersectionality* (Crenshaw 1989, 1991; Collins 2000, 2004; hooks 1981, 1984) is the analytic on which writers need to rely in order to create more comprehensive theoretical frameworks. Intersectionality recognizes that racialized men (especially) were never intended to be said flag bearers or taxpayers within the white nation. Colonized men, although taxed, were not meant to be respectfully or adequately represented. Although, from the beginning, those racialized and colonized were meant to die for the welfare of various empires, the empires never intended to confer rights unto them.

Therefore, any analysis of citizenship, especially *sexual* citizenship, needs to situate the racialization of both citizenship and sexuality. Patricia Hill Collins (2004) outlines the intersections of this form of citizenship with the racialized experience of living in the United States. Her work exposes the undue standard of social regard that black Americans hold in the United States, considering their history of slavery, medical apartheid (a term coined by Harriet A. Washington, 2006),[6] and cultural stereotyping in the present day. To this day, black men are paid less (on average) than white women, incarcerated at purposefully higher rates than any other identity group, and with those accumulated issues, much less likely to be afforded safe and reliable housing. Therefore, the fundamental issues of sexual citizenship are racialized. This relationship to the male counterpart in the racial groups undoubtedly changes what Black women and white women consider feminist political issues. Continuing this narrative, Thaddeus Russell's "The Color of Discipline" (2008) shows the inverse relationship between racial liberation and sexual conservatism. As the "heterosexual family was the most effective vehicle through which to create citizens" (p. 118), Russell argues that the civil rights movement's push for full citizenship abetted conformity to the accepted norms of white sexuality. He shows that, from roughly the 1920s to the 1950s, black culture was largely open to homosexuality and then maps out how movement leaders cloaked themselves in the language of heteronormativity. The movement sacrificed homosexuality in order to "remove the image of black deviancy and show that African Americans could be good citizens" (118). Although these works are geopolitically limited to the recent history of the United States, various works have modeled similar 19th and 20th century citizenship projects elsewhere in the world (Bacchetta and Haritaworn 2011; Epprecht 2005, 2008; Hoad 2007).

Siobhan Somerville (2005) draws attention to the imagined naturalized citizen or person who "desires America," noting that as naturalized means "to make native." The abstract subject, in the US imaginary, is both white and sexually reproductive. M. Jacqui Alexander (2006) navigates this intersection, showing the racial, geographic, political, and classed boundaries that divide access to erotic autonomy. Being a lesbian in Trinidad (made illegal in 1986), and then a Trinidadian lesbian in the United States, (which is rendered illegible due to the whiteness of homosexuality) means living with marginal access to citizenship in both her native state, which proclaimed to be staunchly anti-homosexual, and in her receiving state, which proclaimed staunch acceptance (2006). Her analysis of "crossing" both refers to the transatlantic slave trade, which brought blacks to the Americas and to the boundaries that one disrupts by assuming "contradictory" identities—such as black and lesbian. At the intersection of a marginalized race and a marginalized sexuality, neither state will permit access to full, participatory citizenship.

As colonialism served as the major apparatus to spread Western models of governance, we can witness similar legislative phenomena occurring in formerly colonized regions. The diversity of sexual practices that coexisted before postcolonial transfer of power was often sacrificed to constitute the state (Epprecht 2005). Therefore, regulatory politics of sexuality and gender similar to those in England or the United States (Canaday 2003; Somerville 2005) can be seen in nations across the world (see examples from Epprecht 2005, 2008 and Jeater 2007 for Zimbabwe; Keating 2007 for India; Alexander 2006 for the Caribbean islands; Jayawardena 1986 for the Middle East, Asia, and the Pacific). In regard to gender relations, Kumari Jayawardena (1986) excavates the postcolonial sexual contract while retracing the ways in which the alliance between male and female comrades in several third world independence struggles were severed in the postcolonial nation-building project. For example, Indian politicians entrenched gender inequality through similar legislation to that of their colonial overseers. Contemporarily, Uganda's legislative project of "straightening" citizens can be witnessed through legislative changes in the Penal Code to further define or criminalize sodomy (between 1990 and 2014).

Although the works of Somerville (2005) and Russell (2008) are geopolitically limited to the recent history of the United States, various works have modeled similar 19th and 20th century citizenship projects elsewhere in the world (Bacchetta and Haritaworn 2011; Epprecht 2005, 2008; Hoad 2007). Mark Epprecht (2005) reviews the history of British anti-gay legislation in African colonies. The work not only highlights how hegemonic masculinity (what he calls "the 'cowboy' culture") influenced colonial beliefs of Black incompetency, but also calls for attention to historical missionary attacks on African sexuality and the effects of these attacks on contemporary ideology. As the hegemonic culture of White Rhodesia imposed itself into the African nationalist movement, a movement to "hone" a civilized self-image arose (Jeater 1993; Epprecht 2005).

Various scholarly works reinforce this racialized and sexualized dynamic of the imperial project to "civilize" Africans (Cohen 1970; Stoler 1995, 2002). Becoming more European became an achievement, something accomplishable with the rejection of so-called African perversion. The ethic of independence and restraint is institutionalized as "the price of admission" to citizenship (Russell 2008, p. 124). Therefore, the parameters of citizenship were defined through a moral distancing from African sexuality and an embrace of Victorian gender and labor ideals (Stoler 1995).

When homosexuality is viewed as unproductive and unpatriotic, it becomes inimical to the ethic of self-sacrifice and communal responsibility: the core of citizenship (Russell 2008). The African nation that has internalized the colonial project of sexual restraint sacrifices homosexuality in order to remove the image of black licentiousness. Therefore, homophobic nationalism is useful for reestablishing the communal sensibilities of the true citizen.

Homophobic nationalism stems from a sexual citizenship project of increasing state functionality and national cohesion by propagating a civil fear of homosexuality. This fear not only reproduces normative heterosexuality, it also allows for citizens to band together under one particular patriotic goal: supporting the development of the nation, by calling to attention the problems that would arise with accepting or recognizing any form of homosexuality.

Homonationalism, as developed by Jasbir Puar (2007), describes the process of normativizing homosexuality in a way that advances a nationalist agenda. This homosexuality, similar to the straight state, reproduces the established patterns of consumption and regulation. When granted various civil rights that centralize work ("discrimination") and taxpaying ("marriage") to homosexual nationals, the citizen is able to complement the straight state, rather than contradict it (Puar 2007). Therefore, as the perception of this population grows as an international market (Chasin 2000) and as a diaspora (Puar 1998) it increasingly becomes a state interest to integrate the population into state norms. This interest serves to boost the credibility of the state both on national and international scales, as citizens hold both their own *and* other nations accountable for gay rights. Therefore, the cultural capital that the gay rights movement earns for its constituents fuels homonationalism.

Expanding the theories put forth by sexual citizenry scholars, Puar posits that homonationalism legitimizes dominant states with minimal risk to the state. The United States and other Core countries capitalize on this form of nationalism by strategically deploying the "gay rights" discourse to retain and leverage power over Peripheral nations. Puar juxtaposes the liberal events of gay rights victories in the early 2000s (i.e., the federal overturn of sodomy legislation in 2003) with what she refers to as simultaneous conservative imperial conquests (i.e., the 2003 US invasion of Iraq).

Puar understands categories such as "race" and "gender" as events in this work as they are encounters or experiences with analytic power. She then theorizes the *conviviality* of racial and political events. In particular, she asserts that the conviviality of conservative imperial ventures and the mainstream gay rights undertakings divert attention from the real, racial domination experienced within US borders. The United States turns to celebrate white sexual diversity while it denounces black and brown sexual perversion. Although not explicitly mentioned in her literature, evidence of this is seen through the simultaneity of encouragement for whites to "come out of the closet" and demonization of blacks "on the down low."

White American exceptionalism elevates the experiences of whiteness, while erasing the contributions of all other ethnic or racial groups. This erasure is seen through the ways in which American cultural memory of *Lawrence and Garner v. Texas* actually erases race: as Lawrence is an older white man, and Garner is a young black man. The historic trial became known as *Lawrence v. Texas* through the custom of shortening legal case names. This erasure is more than symbolic; it is a demonstration of the simultaneous process of erasing black experience while using black trauma for the advancement of white citizenry.

The Lasting Importance of Sexual Citizenship Inquiries throughout a Globalized Gay Rights Movement

The increasing inclusion and openness toward gays in a few Western nations does not render sexual citizenship anachronistic. On the contrary, the "increasing inclusion" that we see in some Western nations, and the push for global uniformity in regards to sexual minority rights, reignited the field. In the United States, there is no federal protection from workplace discrimination on the basis of sexual orientation or gender identity. This limits the ability of LGBT people in the country to serve in the public sphere: the crux of citizenship. The marriage debate also settles well into the fold. In fact, the vast majority of "Western" states do not offer full citizenship to gays and lesbians, much less trans and gender non-conforming people outside of these identities. More importantly, Phelan's (2001) theory cites physical safety as the most basic form of citizenship. As trans and queer people of color are harassed, assaulted, and murdered at alarming rates by cisgender, heterosexual males, they are omitted from regular public view.

I connect homophobic nationalism and homonationalism despite their different regional contexts. They are, in this case, reciprocal processes. Also, both rely on racialization processes intended to strengthen their respective nations. Deviant sexual beliefs and practices are connected to globalization and exposure to racial others. In this case, homophobic nationalism in Uganda relies on the assumption that the white or Western foreign agent spreads a destructive sexuality. Homonationalism in the US assumes that there are unproductive ways to be gay (non-monogamous, non-procreative, and non-nationalist). It aligns homonormativity with a national production and securitization. Historically white matters of homosexuality become of national importance, which further erases and problematizes black queerness.

Ultimately, there are several instances of postcolonial amnesia[7] at play, here. Homophobic nationalism relies on a large population forgetting the colonial implications of anti-sodomy legislation. However, it thrives with a memory of the agenda-setting white presence. Homonationalism relies on a large, transnational population forgetting black experience (with sexual demonization, with colonization, with queerness, etc.), but ultimately persisting with blanketed, culturally irrelevant methods of advocacy. In order to navigate this theoretical situation, I've chosen as a case the Anti-Homosexuality Act and the organizing that has occurred in Uganda and between Uganda and the United States.

THE AIMS AND CONTRIBUTIONS OF THIS BOOK

This book offers an investigation that recognizes differentials in autonomy and economic power on each level of interaction. Chapter 1 looks at the domestic relationship between the kuchu rights movement and the anti-gay countermovement. Chapter 2 explores the strategies of invisibility created to navigate the aforementioned relationship, and some of the ways that transnational allies have undermined such strategies. Chapter 3 investigates transnational LGBTI-kuchu relations with an analysis of the advocacy structure developed by Western human rights organizations. Chapter 4 interrogates the narratives of privilege and inequality between kuchu organizers in Kampala. Finally, Chapter 5 provides insight into how and why African-centered activism is underutilized. Overall, this book offers an intentional, multidimensional power critique that aligns with the intersectional feminist imperative developed by scholars such as Kimberle Crenshaw, sociologist Patricia Hill Collins, M. Jacqui Alexander, and Gloria Anzaldúa.

I construct a three-step process to progress this narrative. First, the material and physical presence of foreign governments and transnational NGOs reify nationalist fears of neoimperialism. Secondly, transnational NGOs employ Core-based methodologies to offer liberal grants to those fighting for full sexual citizenship. Then, in the process of embedding small, local movements into large international campaigns, certain activists gain disproportionate material and symbolic compensation. I argue that these dynamics problematize LGBT presence and work: it becomes a regime. Instead of supplying the immediate goods that the kuchu movement demands, such as food, work, shelter, and community, the regime instead redirects the movement and movement-makers toward liberalized, rights-based work, through courts, media, and non-profit organization.

The first process, of anti-gay lawmaking, is explored largely in Chapters 1 and 2. I consider its history, logic, and effects of equal import and therefore attend to each aspect. The physical appearance and representation of Western agency are read as invasion. This reading, in turn, heightens anti-imperial fears and nationalist sentiment. It is inscribed in the very legislation that brought Uganda to the attention of international governments and transnational non-governmental organizations.

Although rights-based work serves an important function in any nation, a model of advocacy that centers liberalized rights does not benefit the majority of kuchus. Unlike high income and/or strongly democratic Core nations, vast underemployment and other economic obstacles in Uganda limit citizens' consumptive and taxpaying capabilities (irrespective of their sexuality) and restrict the political agency of individuals. Therefore, those with already minimal access to economic and political privilege do not reap the benefits of these legal achievements. While earlier chapters set the stage, chapter 3 explains this second process in detail.

The third process, of including kuchus into transnational campaigns, is explored most comprehensively in chapter 4. This advocacy structure creates high profile celebrity-activists, which may limit the movement both by intensifying nationalism and by diverting attention from the general kuchu population in need. The material power provided by regime cooperation becomes an impediment to connecting to the larger citizenry. Therefore, the function of homophobic nationalism is to ensure that (neo)imperial agents do not divide the Ugandan majority. This nationalist discourse may be anti-imperial if it rests on the belief that the gay rights regime seeks to divide a small minority of the population, recast it with a status separate from and superior to the "barbaric other," and then target material support according to this division. All the while, the neo-imperial power economically dominates the entire region and is economically strengthened by this subordination. Following this logic, it should be clear that an interrogation of sexual citizenship matters in the age of homonationalism.

Similarly important is the promotion of a possibility of transnational organizing that does not reproduce hegemonic, imperialist violence. I dedicate an exploration into this possibility in Chapter 5. Chapter 5 serves as a challenge to construct and support queer organizing that combats both the erasure of African Diasporic connections and the anti-black politic inscribed in many of our current international relations.

Altogether, this text interrogates the political economy of international LGBT activism and the effects of such an economy on the queer people living in the cross-section of international power plays and nationalist backlash. *It is a queer time for activism* and thus, an important moment for a sustained look at this very big picture.

NOTES

1. All names in this book are pseudonyms. However, out of respect, Mama is a title that I've used for this woman since growing close to this particular family.

2. Cisgender, or cis, means *not transgender*. The gender that he identifies with normatively aligns with the sex that he was ascribed at birth.

3. The "world system" describes the analysis of the world economy by Immanuel Wallerstein (1974a and b), in which he explains the global division of labor. National contributions to

the world-market are hierarchized. It names predominantly Western nations "the Core" and all others "Semi-Periphery" or "Periphery." The Core's economic power relies on the intentional extraction and devaluation of African resources. The world system perspective reminds us of the parasitic connection that institutions of the West maintain with the Periphery and therefore is favorable to this analysis, over other frames of reference.

4. The East African Community includes the Republics of Burundi, Kenya, Rwanda, South Sudan, Tanzania, and Uganda.

5. I've used data from the Inter-Parliamentary Union of the World Bank to find the average of the EAC and Nordic countries. I included Denmark, Finland, Iceland, Norway, and Sweden in "Nordic Europe."

6. See: Washington, H. A. (2006). *Medical apartheid: The dark history of medical experimentation on Black Americans from colonial times to the present.* Doubleday Books.

7. See Cheney 2012 for an analysis of "postcolonial amnesia" in relation to the argument that protecting Ugandan "cultural tradition" necessitated the Anti-Homosexuality Bill.

Chapter One

Homophobic Nationalism

The Development of Sodomy Legislation

In 2009 the Anti-Homosexuality Bill, often internationally referred to as the Kill the Gays Bill, propelled Uganda to the forefront of global media. [1] The bill earned its international name as reference to the most contentious clause, which would have criminalized "aggravated homosexuality"[2] with the death penalty. After five years, the Bill passed as an Act that omitted the death penalty, but retained life imprisonment for those found guilty of either "the offense of homosexuality" or "aggravated homosexuality."

Within the international media the Anti-Homosexuality Act (AHA) had been framed as a manifestation of natural and timeless African homophobia and yet a surprisingly draconian measure for a country typically concerned with human rights. Although these frames contributed to the sensationalism that garnered the bill international attention, they simultaneously contributed to the international pervasiveness of anti-African xenophobia. Local, Ugandan media understood the AHA as a righteous stance against an "un-African" import: Western sexual deviance (Mwikya 2014; SMUG 2014a). In concert, both local and international media missed the ways in which this form of sexual policing derives from colonial projects of controlling and defining a gendered and racialized African subject. Although references to a monolithic "African" sexuality, sexual culture, and history often go accepted uncritically, numerous scholars have dedicated research to remind us that what is and is not African is contextually based and ever evolving (Epprecht 1998, 2005; Hoad 1999, 2007; Jeater 2007; Khapoya 1994). The continent is home to more than 800 distinctive cultures (Khapoya 1994), each with different sexual histories, practices, rituals, and configurations. Each, perhaps more importantly, with different understandings of what constitutes "sexual." A large body of academic and activist work has contested this "traditional African sexuality" monolith, documenting this extensive history of same sex intimacies and gender nonconformity throughout Africa (Epprecht 1998, 2008; Hoad 2007; Nannyonga-Tamusuza 2002, 2009; Nyanzi 2013; SMUG 2014a; Tamale 2008). Others have demonstrated the cultural means through which this policing was effected (Sadgrove et al. 2012; Stoler 1995, 1997, 2002).

I draw on sexual citizenship literature to show how post-colonial societies developed a model of citizenship largely influenced by the colonial culture of hegemonic masculinity and heterosexuality. Yet, I supplement this literature with homophobic nationalism as an analytical framework, which may help us understand how young nations develop citizenship projects in relation to the struggle for economic independence and sovereignty. I define homophobic nationalism as a state project that propagates a fear of homosexuality among its citizenry in order to cohere a sense of patriotism and bolster belief in the nation's competence and future.

While sexual citizenship theories focus largely on the internal processes of a nation, homophobic nationalism places emphasis on the external, global factors that contribute to the construction of an anti-gay nationalist movement. This chapter contributes a contextualized, legislative case study to a larger body of works that relate to homophobic nationalism (or heteronationalism [Gosine 2009; Lazarus 2011], political homophobia [Weiss and Bosia 2013], the "anti-queer animus" [Thoreson 2014b] or "homosexual panic" [Mwikya 2014]) within African and African Diasporic nation-states. This narrative history of the development of anti-sodomy legislation illuminates the interplay of nationalism with postcolonial anxieties surrounding globalization and the economic vulnerability accompanying development.

Quite differently than other chapters, in which I use ethnography to create a counter-narrative to the oversimplified claims of an innate *African* homophobia, I rely on various qualitative methodologies that demonstrate the ways in which the legislative changes that relate to homosexuality occurred with transnational dialogue and diffusion. Western colonialism created Uganda and the laws that constitute the original penal code; transnational understandings of homosexuality in conversation with neoliberal international programs spurred the various changes to sodomy legislation. Lastly, the AHB and perspectives that developed in support of it arose with struggles for sovereignty in the face of rapid proliferation of NGOs. Therefore, I create a narrative history of the AHA by constructing and contextualizing a timeline of legislative changes to sodomy, beginning with the Ugandan Penal Code of 1950. I offer an analysis of early sodomy legislation, through the development of the AHB and AHA. I triangulate this with parliamentary records from 1999–2014. The data substantiates my analysis of the development of sodomy and homosexuality as a concept and as a threat to Ugandan national interests.

The changes to this Penal Code (in 1990, 2000, and 2005); the Anti-Homosexuality Act both as a drafted bill (2009) and as a passed Act (2014); and several reports documented by social movement organizations in Uganda supplement parliamentary transcripts that I have extracted from the Hansard, the Official Report of the Parliament. The Hansard is the verbatim record of the parliament proceedings and is available online as early as 1993. I searched for records with any of the following words: sodomy, homosexuality, homosexual, anti-homosexuality, gay, lesbian, *kuchu*,[3] Bahati (Anti-Homosexuality Bill author), and Ssempa (well known anti-gay activist), which yielded parliament transcripts from 1999. This methodology supports the analysis of the Anti-Homosexuality Act as a step integrated in an evolutionary development of sodomy legislation, as opposed to an isolated or arbitrary measure in a recent "homophobic wave" (which, as Thoreson [2014b] contests, homogenizes complex, disparate incidences throughout African contexts).

EARLY SODOMY LEGISLATION AND THE MAKING OF DEGENERATE SEXUALITIES (1533–1860)

In 1860, British colonial governors created and enacted Section 377, "unnatural offenses" of the Indian Penal Code (Baudh 2008). This law punished "carnal intercourse against the order of nature with any man, woman or animal" and, for 150 years, did not distinguish between consensual, nonconsensual, adult-adult, or adult-child sexual relationships.[4] These laws spread throughout the Empire at the height of the Victorian era, during which norms of sexual purity and Christian morality were instituted internationally (Baudh 2008). The scale of the reign of the Christian (and British) Empire ensured that these norms and mores reached each corner of the world.

Section 145 of Uganda's criminal code, originally enacted in the last years of the 19th century, is the direct descendent of India's 377. Although Uganda switched from the Indian Penal Code to the Queensland Criminal Code in the 1930s, the latter Code had integrated the same legislation. The blanketed approach to policing sexual practices was thinly veiled. Therefore, when Uganda retained the section "unnatural offenses," it did so with the language that any male commits sodomy when he "has carnal knowledge of any person against the order of nature; has carnal knowledge of an animal; or permits a male person to have carnal knowledge of him against the order of nature" (The Penal Code Act, Section 145).

In 1860, however, the word "homosexuality" did not exist (Katz 1990); as such, today's narrow policing of "homosexual" sex was not entirely relevant at the time. Instead, the government sought to control certain acts (as opposed to groups of people). The action of sodomy, versus the identity of homosexuality, should be understood separately. The language of these laws chooses "debauchery" (Egypt), "buggery" (many Caribbean islands) and "carnal knowledge/intercourse" (such as in India and Uganda) following respective translations of Christian Biblical passages. These terms are now grouped into what we call sodomy. With this and similarly coded language, British colonial law thinly disguised the vast penetration of a completely unified legislative process. Commonwealth Africa and colonies on every other continent were subjected to a cohesive Penal Code.

The novelty and ambiguity of "sodomy" as a term signifies two developments: (1) the codification of particular *illegal*—as opposed to merely inappropriate—behaviors and (2) the mid-20th century specification that these practices are only criminal if they are shared between two people of the same sex. Once a term to combine all non-procreative sexual activity, "sodomy" evolved into a practice shared between people of a particular pathology or disorder. By the mid-19th century, psychiatrists, politicians, and clergymen began to target homosexuality as sodomy in isolation, as opposed to the general understanding of "debauchery" that we see in the language of the 1860 writing of sodomy legislation (Greenberg 2007).

Mark D. Jordan (1997) traces "sodomy" and its pertinence to culture in *The Invention of Sodomy in Christian Theology*. In the 11th century, the Catholic Saint Peter Damian first used Sodomy, as a proper noun, as a term for the actions of Sodomites—the inhabitants of the Biblical city of Sodom (Jordan 1997). Some theologians describe this as gluttonous and playful (non-procreative) sexuality involving men. Jordan (1997) retraces the document which first identifies the practices. He states the following:

> The booklet [by Peter Damian] begins by identifying the [Sodomitic] vice's four species: self-pollution, mutual grasping or rubbing of "manly parts" (*virilia),* pollution "between the thighs" (*inter femora)*, and fornication "in the rear" (*in terga*) (Jordan 1997; 46).[5]

After specifying the practices, Jordan highlights that Damian proceeds to "mock the claim that only those guilty of 'fornication in the rear' should be deposed" (47). This quote directly undermines the contemporary understanding of sodomy that we have reached. This "playful" sexuality refers to releasing sperm anywhere except into a vagina, for procreative purposes, as "pollution." This definition encompassed both same- or other-sex participation.

Jordan continues to trace other theologians who later use the word "sodomy" and the various appropriations they have used for their specific agendas. He argues that, "from the beginning, 'Sodomy' has meant whatever anyone wanted it to mean" (163). It is this abstractive power that allows it to survive as a useful term. The fluidity has since proved particularly useful in courts of law across the world.

England was the first kingdom to create laws against sodomy for its general citizens.[6] The Buggery Act of 1533, enacted by Henry VIII made "buggery" punishable by hanging. Sir William Blackstone, in his *Commentaries on the Laws of England*, notes the following, regarding the "malignity" of sodomy:

> I will not act so disagreeable a part to my readers as well as myself as to dwell any longer upon a subject the very mention of which is a disgrace to human nature. It will be more eligible to imitate in this respect the delicacy of our English law, which treats it, in its very indictments, as a crime not fit to be named." (Blackstone 1916: 2422)

Blackstone continues to assure that the most severe punishments may be issued to perpetrators (and "consenting parties") for a crime not to be named among Christians (p. 2422–2423). This revisits the ambiguity Jordan alludes to and demonstrates the power of conviction with which lawmakers and commentators disapprove of these crimes.

The British kingdom was not alone for long. France, too, enacted anti-sodomy laws until Napoleon amended them to solely criminalize rape in 1791, and then abolished legislation using the term sodomy altogether in 1806 (Kirby 2011). Prussia—the Christian kingdom controlling mostly modern Germany until 1947—had proposed a law against "unnatural fornication" in 1852 (Johansson and Percy 2006). This law included sex "between males" or of "human and beast." The Nazi regime intensified this law, resulting in the conviction, castration, and/or murder of thousands of men in the 1930s (Plant 1986).

The Victorian era, the period in which Uganda became a colony of Great Britain, solely embraced sexuality within the context of procreation between two married individuals. Accordingly, as seen today, although cultural marriages allow polygyny, marriage with official, legal recognition is between a man and a woman. Laws that guide relationships and procreation remain an especially relevant and acceptable means to control sexuality. The Victorian project focused on ruling bodies *and* minds: actions and ideology.

Controlling degenerate or pagan sexualities on the continent proved an important mission for white colonial authority (Stoler 1997). Civilizing natives allowed for a more subservient demographic, which in turn aided Europeans in fulfilling their preordained mission to expand. The colonizers' Christian beliefs also backed legislation ensuring that Africans and whites did not have sex, so that they did not breed a race that would challenge the racial hierarchies. In this way, the projects of African Christianity and colonialism developed along similar paths, both securing the other's prevalence.

Policing gender and sexuality through the institutions of marriage and family proved a crucial precondition to stabilizing colonialism. In particular, the European formation of capitalist nation-states relies on a masculinity that privileges attaining financial resources. These resources serve the dual purposes of contributing to the reconstitution of the state—the public– and the home—the private. These domains of social life change the applicability of sodomy and degeneracy; which signifies the classed and raced understanding of proper sexuality as well as the differences in policing that one experienced due to their race and class.

THE CLASSED AND RACED IMPLICATIONS OF APPROPRIATE SEXUALITY (1899–1950)

The land area now called Uganda was comprised of multiple kingdoms, then taken over by force by the British in 1888 (officially in 1894), and as of 1962 considered one independent nation. Racist colonial ideation allowed for the rest of the world to render a very essentialized idea of the multiple ethnicities within this colony (and the continent, at large). The "native," in this sense, became every non-white person in any given area. Due to the indirect rule of the British, these "natives" would be governed as a group of non-citizens (workers) until 1962.[7] That is to say, they would never be integrated into British citizenship. They, instead, *became* Ugandans.

In this sense, what is now accepted as Ugandan or African follows a relatively short (120 year) construction. Indeed, colonialism constructed the dichotomized race relations to which the world commonly refers. Although the relationship of colonizer/colonized is often reduced to a racially white/black divide, there continue to exist many ethnicities, cultures, and languages in Uganda, many of which experienced colonial authority very differently (Doornbos 1976).

For example, the British used ethnic stratification purposefully. The cultural diversity in Uganda allowed for the British to pick and choose the most collaborative races. The Bahima, at the end of the 19th century was a group of pastoralists, accustomed to extended social networks and the hierarchy of chiefdom. Therefore, although they were a numerical minority in Ankole (a district of Uganda), they were chosen disproportionately as administrators in the region, once colonized. The British identified them as "born gentlemen" and a "superior race" (563) to the neighboring Bairu, who were farmers. The British favored what they identified as the collaborative essence of the Bahima culture and then recruited them into a disproportionate number of leadership positions in order to assume indirect rule (566). In this structure where no ethnic rivalry existed between the two groups, the British merged various ethnicities into a blanket race, and then constructed intergroup hierarchies.

Similarly, in Buganda, the neighboring kingdom, this process of hierarchical recruitment ensured the political domination by the Baganda people over other clans in the district. Baganda culture, in particular, stressed an ethos of individualism and the benefits of empire (Khapoya 1994; Mukuthuria 2006). As the British used indirect rule to use native leaders as proxies for British regulation, they relied on a system that could reinforce ethnic stratification while giving the appearance of valorizing Ugandan leadership. Therefore, by 1901, the Baganda were recruited into the Ankole district to assume leadership positions. By 1907, of 74 chieftainships in Ankole, the Bahima had 30 positions; the Baganda had 22 (Doornbos 1976, p. 560). Although both of these groups constituted numerical minorities, they were determined to have character traits most readily transferrable to the needs of British imperialism.

This formation created a stratification system that would last throughout Uganda's history as a colony. So although Ugandans could not achieve similar social standing to the British, certain sociocultural characteristics created a conduit for the transfusion of European values. Particularly for those categorized as men, this conduit provided a template for social mobility in the colony that would later continue in postcolonial formations. Because of indirect rule, "native men" could aspire to positions of leadership and public service to the colony. Indirect rule transferred the message that one could transcend his primitive ethnicity, and become a loyal servant of the colony, with certain sexed, classed, and economic aspirations. Most notably, the transcendence involved the imperative to subordinate his newly gendered, native woman counterpart.

Great Britain enacted policies in each colony in order to repress sexual expression. The strategies of domination that transferred Victorian morality extend to all former British colonies of Africa (Cage and Evans 2003; Epprecht 2005; Gupta 2008; Stoler 2002). Although each colony differed, the British compensated with regionally structured organizations and overarching ideals for all of the Empire. The population of white settlers or the severity with which the British ruled might vary, but the project was the same throughout the colonies: civilize Africans in the image of the "proper Brit" and extract the resources of their land and labor.

White power existed as the only legitimate power in the colonies. European authority reinforced the division of labor by the valuation of those most "civilized" and the denigration of those most "uncivilized": whiteness and the ability to approximate it constitute the former. An analysis of socioeconomic status only furthers our understanding of the illusory application of civility. The acquisition of European goods became signs of class and value, leading African men to aspire to afford them (Epprecht 2005; Newbury

1998). In this way, material culture and status coalesced as a strong impetus for "betterment." Combining material status, proper religious affiliation, and education, an African man could aspire for position or favor in his locality, even if he would never "achieve" a British identity (Doornbos 1976; Stoler 1997).

The project of colonization is necessarily a gendered one. Betterment, superiority, and authority all existed as gendered configurations: governing subjects was a *man's job,* and colonization introduced the particularities of this gendering system (Oyēwùmí 2005). In training, or "bringing" the African male to the status of a *man,* British figures sharpened a monolithic image of their masculinity (Stoler 1997). This masculinity, which presupposes heterosexuality, demands the acquisition of materials and status. Its valuation played a strong role in the adoption of European ideals and rejection of deviant or "feminine" sexualities (Epprecht 2005). For "real" men, this status also requires distancing oneself from primitivity and blackness—and as such, taking on the identity of the ruling class becomes a multifaceted task.

The Queensland Code of 1899, the standard penal code that the protectorate adopted in the 1930s, defines a private act as any of the following:

(a) showering or bathing; or
(b) using a toilet; or
(c) another activity when the person is in a state of undress; or
(d) intimate sexual activity that is not ordinarily done in public.

The Code renders these private acts illegal when committed publically. Although *de jure* sodomy can be committed in public or in private, according to the Ugandan Penal Code Act of 1950, sexual activity is only legal when committed as a private act. Sodomy heightens state policing and renders the idea of the private meaningless. Sodomy, referred to as the "unnatural offense" in the Penal Code, becomes spectacle. Enforcing anti-sodomy legislation, therefore, becomes a matter of keeping the public in order.

However, various economic factors contribute to whether or not one can access the "private" in order to engage in sexual activity. Said otherwise, one must contribute to the public sphere—the sphere that, for reasons stated earlier, is largely denied to nonwhites and people of sexes other than male. With the exception of those few African males who had already ascended into the proxy leadership positions, most Africans could not afford their own property. Those who cannot afford to access privacy become degenerates whenever they act sexually. In this sense, sexual morality serves as much of a classed and raced distinction.

Native became analogous to degenerate and therefore harmful to nationality or civility. This analogue substantiated active policing through legislative and cultural means. Therefore, as historically demonstrated (Epprecht 1998 is one such work)[8] when labor divides align with racial difference, the powerless grow to be perceived as the bearers of lawlessness, and the hands of the law are disproportionately applied to nonwhite bodies.

CONTINUING SEXUAL POLICING AS AN "INDEPENDENT" NATION (1962–2008)

When Milton Obote assumed his position as prime minister in 1962, the mere weeks that had led up to independence had accommodated virtually no change to the Ugandan Penal Code; colonial constructions of criminality remained in tact. Both Idi Amin and Milton Obote's disregard for the Western model of homophobic nationalism, for using legislation to police sexuality, may be symbolized through the lack of changes to sodomy legislation during their combined, 24-year reign. There also may not have been the necessary political climate, globally and locally, for the prioritization of such legislation. Although the gay rights movement had begun in the United States and in Great Britain, there is no evidence that Amin or Obote were concerned with these changes. Instead, national cohesion occurred through an authoritarian regime maintained through both strategic and arbitrary violence. Intricate policy changes were rather unimportant before what Aili Mari Tripp (2004) refers to as the "softening" of authoritarianism in Africa. Anti-sodomy legislation in Uganda remained unchanged from colonial periods, until 1990, at which time Yoweri Museveni had four years of service as the president.

In 1990, Ugandan legislators began to respark the homophobic nationalist project in response to the HIV/AIDS crisis and the diffusion of homophobic policies of the United States. Uganda fronted as Africa's success story for its aggressive response and reported reduction of HIV/AIDS prevalence. Two unfortunate realities coexist with these tactics. First, the reduction of prevalence has been shown to result, at least in part, from the high number of AIDS related deaths and unreliable sampling in the southern and urban regions (Parkhurst 2002). Secondly, and most relevant, the ABC program (Abstinence, Be faithful, and use Condoms) paralleled an attack on the LGBT population.

Although homosexual sex was not as strong a local factor in the spread of HIV, the US association of the two affected much of the world. In 1990, Uganda strengthened the penalty for committing sodomy to life imprisonment (Gupta 2008; Hollander 2009). Advancing and reinforcing anti-sodomy legislation became a pre-emptive strike, a way for the government to ensure that its people did not engage in this sexual deviance. Importantly, however, as Ugandan policymakers witnessed this messaging that "sodomy" leads to a particularly aggressive mode of transmission, creating this legislation signaled a continuation of their equally aggressive campaign to end HIV/AIDS.

Over a decade later, in 2003, Honorary Jane Alisemera reported the following to parliament:[9]

> As we fight AIDS, we know very well that AIDS spreads fast through homosexuality, through the anal canal. Even as Ugandans, as Africans, we have never promoted homosexuality. You would look at homosexuality like you look at a goat and a human being. I want to tell you that in this era of AIDS, we should stop talking about homosexuality and we only concentrate on prevention of AIDS through the heterosexual route rather and not the anal route.

Alisemera's comments have two potential implications. The first is that policymakers offered a disproportionate amount of attention to homosexuality as a scapegoat. Being tough on sexual vices would not only strengthen their reputation as aggressive fighters against HIV, but it could also allow them to appear strong despite losing the battle against heterosexual transmission—the main mode in Uganda. The second implication is that talk about homosexuality had to be silenced in order for them to honestly reassert control of the spread of HIV. These indications need not be mutually exclusive.

In fact, Uganda began to combat HIV by refusing health care to anyone who admitted to having a same sex sexual relationship. Sexual Minorities Uganda, the primary organization for same-gender loving and gender nonconforming (SGL and GNC) Ugandans has reported how the Ugandan health-care system became openly hostile as a result of this anti-gay rhetoric (2005). The misguided argument that LGB people contract HIV through illegal activity and therefore need not be treated directly conflicts with the fact that even intravenous drug users and inmates are eligible for treatment (as reported by SMUG 2005). The stigmatization set by the US that regards homosexuality as a *cause* for the disease complicated the process of treatment for SGL and GNC people in Uganda.

This history of the Ugandan HIV/AIDS politics and policies plays an important role in the empirics of the Anti-Homosexuality Act. As the 1990 change to life-imprisonment for a sodomy offense came on the heels of HIV/AIDS politics, one must recognize that regardless of whether or not Ugandans consider it a "gay disease" (and they do not), the discussion of homosexuality (such as that which Alisemera wanted to end) did affect politics. The Anti-Homosexuality Act passed with a clause that ensured that if one has "homosexual sex" while living with HIV, they would be charged with aggravated homosexuality. Therefore, recognizing the complex interplay of HIV status and identity is crucial to understanding the changes in sodomy legislation.

The next development in sodomy legislation occurred a decade afterward. The Penal Code Amendment (Gender References) Act of 2000 revised the "unnatural offenses" for gender-neutral language (such as "any person" instead of any male, and "him or her"). This change, which extended throughout the Penal Code, effectively criminalized female-female sex. The feminist organizations behind this act intended to foster gender equity in the law by de-gendering the pronouns used. Therefore, sodomy, assault, or rape, which at one point could only be perpetrated by males, could now occur between "a person" and "him or her"—allowing legal recognition of victims or perpetrators of any sex or gender. This gender ambiguity, however, effectively sparked the beginning of legal recognition of lesbian sex. Therefore this feminist act, ironically, realized equality as the ability to penalize a woman the same way as a man, in terms of the law.

TOWARD "COMPREHENSIVE MEASURES": DEVELOPING THE ANTI-HOMOSEXUALITY ACT (2009–2014)

The interpretive flexibility of the language in the Ugandan Penal Code Act of 1950, which remained after independence, allowed for the penalization of an array of same sex intimacies. Until the passage of the Anti-Homosexuality Act (February 2014) and after it was annulled (in August 2014), Uganda could recognize an unnatural offense as any "carnal knowledge of any person [or animal] against the order of nature." This offense, as previously stated, was already punishable by life imprisonment. Sections 146 and 148 of the Penal Code also sentenced those who commit acts of gross indecency and those who *attempt* (unsuccessfully) to commit unnatural offenses with up to seven years of imprisonment. Acts of gross indecency are understood as intimate practices that fall short of sex; therefore, the code leaves room for interpretation meanwhile casting a large net for criminal actions.

Chapter XIV of 120, titled "Offenses against morality," hosted the various sections regarding sodomy. The ambiguous wording, "carnal knowledge," "indecent practices," "[gross] acts" allowed for legal reconfiguration. Instead of criminalizing unnatural actions, Uganda shifted into criminalizing groups or identities considered gross or unnatural. This reconsideration occurred interactively, with a global sphere that created transnational identities such as *lesbian* or *gay*. For this reason, a law that used to target a particular set of actions—actions connected to non-procreative (and therefore immoral) sex—morphed into laws targeting a particular set of "immoral" people. The other "immoral" people included in this chapter of the Penal Code are rapists, the incestuous, zoosexuals, and child molesters.

Although the slippery wording of the code allows for the penalization of a larger breadth of acts, it also, counterproductively, has a weak enforcement mechanism. From the perspective of the anti-gay mobilizers and parliamentarians, the criminal code was "defected" and in need of a reformation.

> All this time that we have had these laws in place, have we successfully even prosecuted two people who have been engaged in homosexuality or has the whole set of laws in place been a failure? If they are a failure, it is very urgent that we immediately change these laws to address the need of our society. We need to prosecute people who are contaminating the African society. We have cultural values that we have to protect
> (Ms. Beatrice Anywar Atim, FDC, Woman Representative, Kitgum, April 2009).

For Section 145, one must be caught in the act or confess to having had consensual gay or lesbian sex. For clear reasons, the judiciary had difficulty sentencing those who had been arrested. As the wording exists currently, due to the unlikelihood of an official confession, there would need to be concrete evidence, procured through methods such as sleeping with a suspect in order to convict him/her (McClelland 2012; Tamale 2009). Therefore, no one in Uganda's postcolonial history had been sentenced for sodomy before the AHB. Instead, anti-sodomy legislation had been used more as a tactic of terror—to arrest suspected deviants, put them in holding, harass, torture, or blackmail SGL and GNC Ugandans (SMUG 2014b). The enforcement has been entirely extrajudicial, in the sense of outside of courts.

The reformation, the "comprehensive measures" that many within the parliament had hoped for aims to strengthen the enforcement mechanisms. The Anti-Homosexuality Act ensured measures that would 1) protect the sovereignty of Uganda against globalizing forces; 2) inoculate impoverished citizens against homosexual bribery; and 3) end the progress that the sexual justice organizations had begun to make. Therefore, the AHA has a section on the "Promotion of Homosexuality" to specifically accomplish each.

The AHA began as what was commonly referred to as the "Kill the Gays Bill." The intention behind the draft was to distinguish sodomy from other "unnatural offenses," define and punish "aggravated homosexuality" with the death penalty, and increase the enforcement mechanism so that citizens could hold other citizens and NGOs accountable for preventing the spread of gay positive messages. Ugandan parliamentarians and anti-gay mobilizers alike had been noting the presence of openly homosexual citizens, organizations by and for kuchu Ugandans, and foreign NGOs that promote safe-sex practices and cultural empowerment for SGL and GNC Ugandans. Section 13, "Promotion of Homosexuality" disallows a) the flow of gay pornography; b) funds to sponsor the promotion of same sex sexual acts; c) offering a premise for same sex sexual acts to occur within; d) browsing gay pornography; or e) acting as an accomplice or abetting related practices. If a person were to be found guilty of Promotion, they could be fined up to 100,000,000

UG shillings (nearly 40,000 US dollars), or serve between 5 to 7 years in jail, or be both fined and imprisoned. If an NGO or a corporate body is found guilty of Promotion, the business certificate of registration will be canceled and the director may serve seven years in jail.

The bill especially attended to nongovernmental organizations. As anti-gay members of parliament consider health-care services for LGBT people "recognition of such sexual relations," the introduction of this bill further diminished the relatively inexistent HIV/AIDS care available for SGL or GNC Ugandans (SMUG 2005). A health-care provider's aid to a gay person that does not lead to an arrest could potentially count as "aiding and abetting" or "failure to disclose" a homosexual, which the bill makes illegal. Clause 7 of Part II states that "a person who aids, abets, counsels or procures another to engage in acts of homosexuality commits an offense and is liable on conviction to imprisonment for seven years"; clause 14 of the same Part penalizes the failure to disclose with a fine or a sentence of less than three years. Although this bill had not yet passed, the threat alone furthered the severe decline in willingness to treat homosexual patients that began immediately after the conference (HRW 2014).

Creating this crime of Promotion of Homosexuality attended to the cries of parliamentarians who had expressed anger about the open presence of LGBTI and/or kuchu identified organizers for years before drafting the bill. Between 2003 and 2009, parliamentarians discussed their concern of the effect created by kuchu organizers when they cooperate with richer nations or INGOs. Repeatedly, they mentioned that these organizations were gaining more support and visibility with the effort. The clause on the "Promotion of Homosexuality" would ensure that citizens reported known homosexuals, for fear of prosecution through alliance. This clause would send the message that the country was serious about preserving heterosexual norms.

> I rise on a matter of public concern. Today in the *New Vision* newspaper, there was an article with the headline, *Donors want Gay rights* . . . This information was given by the Executive Director of Foundation for Human Rights Initiative, Mr Livingstone Sewanyana. He said that donors are currently pressurising Uganda to legalise homosexuality.
>
> Mr Speaker, I do not have to read the whole article, but the same article continues to say that recently, Ugandan homosexuals submitted to donors a proposal of US$1 million for mass mobilisation. . .
>
> We know very well that the religious people here have condemned homosexuality, and we know it is against our culture. Now I am calling upon this august House to condemn this act. (*Applause*)
>
> —Mr. Henry Basaliza Araali, MP, Fort Portal Municipality, November 2003

> Homosexuality was unheard of; today we have a section of our people who are pushing for homosexuals to be defended, that the law must be in place that provides for people to enjoy the freedom to exercise homosexuality.
>
> —Dr. James Nsaba Buturo, former Minister of State for Ethics and Integrity in the Office of the Vice President, July 2006

> Madam Speaker, I rise on a point of national importance. In today's *New Vision*, there is a front page picture showing gay activists addressing a press conference. To the best of my knowledge, homosexuality is illegal. I know that our cultural norms, our religious norms, and even our Constitution do not allow homosexuality. However, these people have now been given the opportunity to address press conferences.
>
> —Mr Latif Sebaggala, DP, Kawempe Division North, April 2009

These statements, each made three years apart, were embedded in larger discussions in parliament regarding the economic power of kuchus and their newfound, foreign allies. The three quoted parliamentarians have spoken extensively about homosexuality for years prior and post these dates. Dr. Buturo, the former Minister for Ethics and Integrity, was a particularly charged leader against homosexuality, and this position—now chaired by Simon Lokodo—has since continued the anti-homosexual strengthening. Sebaggala rallied parliamentarians and gathered signatures to reignite the Anti-Homosexuality Act after it was repealed in 2014. However, rather than isolated commentary, these emerge from the questioning of Ugandan lawmakers into the cultural and economic capital of some kuchu organizations.

Western donors are seen to have unlimited resources for the particular issues that they value, issues such as homosexuality are imagined to receive more finances than poverty or hunger, which creates resentment within the majority. The same donors are also imagined as responsible for the spotlighting of such activists, organizing press conferences and media appearances. These comments demonstrate a linear progression in LGBT activism—from rumors of an organization attempting to form and mobilize in 2003; to a section of people visibly advocating for LGBTI rights; to an internationally recognized conference organization holding press conferences in 2009. This linear progress, however, led to the validation of parliamentarians' earliest concerns: the cultural capital of international LGBTI organizing could lead to significant changes in Ugandan civil society. The first decade of the 2000s featured exactly that—behind the scenes growth of kuchu acceptance.

Ugandan parliamentarians sought legislative redress to this damage. They intended the "Promotion of Homosexuality" clause as this redress. The Promotion of Homosexuality criminalizes the work of international organizations in Uganda, that fund and train domestic organizations to advocate for safe sex practices. It also creates a nationalist unity against homosexuality, and legally ensures the buy in and participation of regular citizens. This has been a major political motivation of the first of these featured parliamentarians, Henry Basaliza Araali, who also stated in 2005 that this form of nationalism draws "tangible development." When citizens can unify under specific moral and cultural values, the economy benefits.

Importantly, it was in 2005 that Uganda passed the Prohibition of Same-Sex Marriages. Although such unions were already "unlawful"—or not recognized by the state—the prohibition explicitly criminalized them in July with a vote of 111 For—17 Against—3 Abstentions. This prohibition became Article 31 (2)(a) of the constitution. Although this is not a clause related to unnatural offenses, it is particularly curious in that it exists simultaneously with already significant sodomy laws. A country, one that already regards same-sex sexual activity as criminal, felt the need to specify that same sex marriages would be unlawful. The logic behind this vote proved Ugandan lawmakers' omnipresent fear of cultural globalization. The Western struggle for gay marriage proved meaningful enough for the parliament to enact this overstatement, reaffirming their anti-gay and simultaneously anti-Western stance. This dual purpose concretizes homophobic nationalism, as lawmakers enact legislation in order to preserve "Ugandan morality" in the wake of what is understood as a growing Western influence. This action exposes the true nature of the nationalist logic, as anti-homosexuality endeavors come to proxy as anti-globalization actions.

The attempt to expand jurisdiction (Part IV, 16) and apply extradition (Part IV, 17) in the bill shows another important move toward "comprehensive measures." Clause 16(a)-*Extra-Territorial Jurisdiction* proposes to apply the AHA "to offenses committed outside Uganda" if one person is a Ugandan national. This clause was debated and retracted shortly before the passage of the bill into an Act, because the parliamentarians in attendance believed they wouldn't have the power to enforce it. However, this attempt indicates parliamentarian's anxieties about emigration—long-term exposure to Western-ness—or shorter-term travel and the need to hold Ugandan nationals accountable for protecting the sexual politic while abroad.

ANTI-IMPERIALISM AND THE IMPORTATION OF HOMOSEXUALITY TO VULNERABLE PEOPLES

When originally drafted, the Anti-Homosexuality Bill opened with the principle and objectives; made an effort to define homosexuality both in its standard and "aggravated" forms and related offenses; and then followed with changes to jurisdiction. The following is excerpted from the principle of the original Anti-Homosexuality Bill:

Textbox 1.1: The Principle. Sectioned from the original draft of the Bahati bill

1.1. The principle

The object of this Bill is to establish a comprehensive consolidated legislation to protect the traditional family by prohibiting (i) any form of sexual relations between persons of the same sex; and (ii) the promotion or recognition of such sexual relations in public institutions and other places through or with the support of any Government entity in Uganda or any non governmental organisation inside or outside the country.

This Bill aims at strengthening the nation's capacity to deal with emerging internal and external threats to the traditional heterosexual family.

This legislation further recognises the fact that same sex attraction is not an innate and immutable characteristic.

The Bill further aims at providing a comprehensive and enhanced legislation to protect the cherished culture of the people of Uganda; legal, religious, and traditional family values of the people of Uganda against the attempts of sexual rights activists seeking to impose their values of sexual promiscuity on the people of Uganda.

There is also need to protect the children and youths of Uganda who are made vulnerable to sexual abuse and deviation as a result of cultural changes, uncensored information technologies, parentless child developmental settings and increasing attempts by homosexuals to raise children in homosexual relationships through adoption, foster care, or otherwise.

The Principle elucidates the mobilizers' anti-imperialist standpoint. It introduces the "external threats" of people who seek to "impose their values of sexual promiscuity on the people of Uganda." Noting that those people are in direct opposition with the people of Uganda highlights that the bill opposes the efforts of various, foreign peoples and organizations with the power to *impose* an ideology contrary to conservative religious mores. As the

Principle points out, these threatening agents operate through public institutions, NGOs, and even possibly with the cooperation of the Ugandan government (ii). This ambitious bill would prohibit all forms of support and recognition of a homosexual populace.

The following extracts demonstrate the discussion held among parliamentarians, which strongly focused on protecting the youth and impoverished:

> I would like to see, among the penalties that a homosexual practitioner should get, an addition to the already existing penalty of life imprisonment. Since we still have the death penalty, we should actually condemn these people to death because they are killing our children and actually desirous of exterminating Ugandans. They just want to come and occupy this land.
>
> —Grace Oburu, NRM, Woman Representative, Tororo, April 2009

> I think it is very important for Government to create jobs for the youth. This is because poverty drives the youth to receive money from these agents in exchange for recruitment into homosexuality.
>
> —Santos Piro, Independent, East Moyo, Adjumani, April 2009

The claim that foreign funds promote homosexuality among youth relates to the idea that recruitment takes place in classrooms and organizations. Western sponsorship of homosexuality encompasses gay-straight alliances, curricula that include homosexuality, and internationally funded scholarships for African LGBT identified students. A guest writer for the *Observer* fervently supports the Anti-Homosexuality Bill for the belief that a highly funded gay student organization at Makerere University secretly bribes students into engaging in or publically supporting homosexuality. He asserts that the organization serves as a "blatant attempt at whitewashing homosexuality and brainwashing Ugandan university students who ordinarily might be turned off by the vice" (Jabo 2011).

Government actors believe that economic devastation exacerbates vulnerability to the spread of homosexuality. Therefore, they imagine themselves as "courageous" and responsible defenders of the people against the threat that powerful, wealthy nations wish to impose. Equally, many believe that individuals in more economically empowered positions are protected from the vice. In December 2013, as parliament finally debated the bill, MP Katoto rose to object to Prime Minister Mbabazi, exclaiming, "*Our kids are not protected, yours are protected because they move with escorts. Do you want other people to sodomise. . .*"[10] before the chairperson interrupted him. This belief that money can protect individuals from homosexuality invokes a counterintuitive logic when one considers that "the West" is understood as the agent of homosexuality and the most economically empowered. However, it exposes the firmness of the belief that some hold that Africans, at their most natural state of being, are heterosexual. Notably, many people who support anti-homosexuality measures do not necessarily believe this, such as President Museveni himself, who in 1999 spoke of the *ebitingwa* (homosexuals) in Ankole, who existed without exposure to or interaction with Westerners.

Along those lines, the March 2009 seminar "Exposing the Truth Behind Homosexuality and the Homosexual Agenda" in Kampala occurred in effort to restore "traditional" Ugandan values by blocking the importation of Western homosexuality. Framing homosexuality as a symptom of American moral decline, American evangelicals pushed for awareness of the global gay agenda (Kaoma 2009). These preachers framed the West—the United States included—as a battleground lost, arguing that only a small minority of Americans are true Christians. Uganda is imagined as much more devout and faithful to the scripture; therefore, although in colonial and perhaps precolonial narratives Christianity and "the West" went hand in hand, an anti-Western stance now can be taken by resisting Western (atheist) decadence. Although the American evangelists have since taken various positions to distance themselves from the bill, the conference and its speakers played a crucial role in popularizing support for the bill (Kaoma 2009), as well as the anti-globalization framing of homophobic mobilization in Uganda.

As the data within this chapter show, these particular American evangelicals were neither the impetus nor innovators of the anti-gay fervor. However, the presence of American "testimonials" against American moral decline garnered additional popular support throughout Kampala. It also spurred continuous debate in parliament leading up to the proposal of the bill, creating a consistency that cannot be witnessed in the years before the seminar (conversed April 1, April 6, April 15, and April 29).

Framing the "homosexual agenda" as moral decline backed by rich Whites had begun long before this conference, as shown earlier by the 2006 quotation from the Minister of State for Ethics, Dr. Buturo. Thoroughly sensationalized, international media centered the American evangelical involvement in the creation of this bill, which in turn allowed for outraged, American attention specifically to those evangelicals. This attention, however, led to the dehistoricization of anti-sodomy legislation in Uganda, as most reports did not even mention the life imprisonment penalty already on the books. The media ultimately contributed to the egregious missteps in international relations that led to sanctions, aid cuts, and other fuel to the anti-imperialist fire. It did not attend to the ways in which the global, political economy influenced the legislation and led lawmakers to gather their collective upset at homosexuality for so many years prior to the bill.

Altogether, the conflation of LGBTI organizing in Uganda with Western donor support—and therefore, economic power—set the stage for anti-imperial argumentation. As homosexuality became imagined as a heavily financed vice, imposed upon a Christian and heterosexual nation, it became reasoned as imperial. This began slowly, but we can witness it as early as in 2003—when Integrity Uganda attempted to register as an NGO and Araali spoke in parliament about the possibility of a "mass mobilization of homosexuals" supported by $1m USD. The international responses to the AHB and then AHA aggravated this tension.

In response to the proposal of the bill, a number of Western nations preemptively spoke out against Uganda. The Swedish Development Assistance minister Gunilla Carlsson threatened to withdraw the annual $50 million of aid that Sweden lends Uganda. A number of European countries mirrored this threat. British Prime Minister David Cameron followed, albeit sluggishly, and two years later joined the other nations in "reconsidering" its aid policy in the case of Uganda, if the country did not rescind the bill (BBC 2011). After the passage of the AHA, the World Bank and several European countries cut, postponed, or redirected between US$110–140 million in loans to Uganda.

The threats to cut aid worked, counterproductively, to the benefit of the anti-gay fervor. This response could have been preempted, as it aligns with the 2003 statement by MP Dombo Lumala who, in response to global recognition of same sex marriage said that the government should mobilize the people of Uganda so that "under no circumstances shall the donors intimidate [them]."[11] Economic threats cause a reactive mobilization. In December 2009, after the Swedish government delivered their warning, Ugandan parliamentarians responded by announcing the necessity of passing the bill "expeditiously" and "head on," rather than reconsidering the anti-gay stance itself.[12] Threats intensify self-righteous anti-imperialism; they restate a definitive understanding of economic power in global, political relationships.

Parliamentarians, including the Speaker of the House Rebecca Kadaga, note that if President Museveni were to veto the bill, he would do it based off of Western cultural values, essentially because Western nations would *pay for him to do so.* This response echoed throughout Ugandan anti-gay segments of society, and resparked the frame that Uganda must not be made vulnerable to foreign investment in homosexuality due to their economic situation. After receiving reports from Ugandan scientists that there has been no proof in the science community that homosexuality is immutable, genetic, or biological, President Museveni signed the legislation (Kasasira 2014). At the public signing, he declared his action to be in opposition to Western cultural imposition, stating the following:

> We have been disappointed for a long time by the conduct of the West, the way you conduct yourselves there. . . . Our disappointment is now exacerbated because we are sorry to see that you live the way you live, but we keep quiet

> about it. Now you say 'you must also live like us'—that's where we say no (Karimi and Thompson 2014).

The conflicting international and domestic pressures gave way to two developments: first, Museveni signed the legislation that he originally opposed and soon after, the AHA was nullified. Although, officially, a lack of quorum when voting on the legislation led to the nullification, many supposed that the international attention was truly responsible. Worth noting here, however, is that regardless of this responsibility, the government is able to continue to appear to its supporters as maintaining the moral high ground and fortitude to fight a corrupt, global political system. Responding internationally to this in a way that dislocates the importance of that message also dislocates the SGL and GNC Ugandans who have come to embody this political-economic tension. In order to effect change for the safety of kuchu Ugandans, international advocates must reach away from quick power plays and toward an understanding of this history.

CONCLUSION

Lawmaking against homosexuality in Uganda has evolved alongside anti-globalization and anti-imperialist imaginings. The conversations surrounding uncensored information technologies or cultural flows arise from the effort to mitigate the perceived harms of globalization. On the other hand, legislators evoke imperialism when they discuss the coupling of Western economic power with an imposition of subversive activities in the country. This relies on a fear of either covert or overt supplanting of the cultural, economic, or social mores of the country through INGO funding or leveraging aid. This chapter has explored both impetuses as they relate to nation-building and nationalism, or citizens' cultural identification with the governing state.

Young states, such as Uganda, a country only around fifty years old, struggle immensely with nation-building as a project. As the process of "making the state straight" (Canaday 2009) proves integral to the Western model of nation-building, I have shown how homophobic nationalism, a nationalism that literally fears incorporating homosexuality, exists in Uganda, in a historically contingent way. The interplay between state action and the action of civil society in the formation of the heterosexual state has developed from a model of nationalism bestowed upon Uganda during the colonial project. This model marries heterosexuality with economic development and invulnerability, and is imagined to serve nationalist cohesion.

The narrative that I have developed describes the co-constitutive natures of ethnicity, sexuality, and development. In the postcolonial context, as M. Jacqui Alexander observes, "Not just (any) body can be a citizen any more, for some bodies have been marked by the state as non-procreative, in pursuit of sex only for pleasure, a sex that is non-procreative of babies and of no economic gain" (Alexander 1994, p. 6). Citizenship in colonies was built upon a "template" meant to dignify and imitate the "white bourgeois heterosexual man"; it is now, in Alexander's words, in its black male "configuration" (p. 35). Ugandan sexual citizenship is imagined as "black masculine men whose sole sexual desire is for their black feminine women" (Nyanzi 2014, p. 34).

I continue and expand upon this understanding of homophobic nationalism. It is the process of dejecting homosexuality, feminine masculinities, and other formations that subvert the masculine nation (such as individualism, polyandry, and masculine femininities). Upholding the masculine nation is a priority for nations seeking to reproduce their cultural values, social standing, and economic virility. Homophobic nationalism, in this way, is a model begun by Western empires and continued through the legacies of those countries colonized by such empires in the 20th century. The development of the AHA demonstrates the continuation of two unfortunate colonial legacies: first, the "civilizing" of African sexuality through conformity to the heterosexist gender binary in the colonial order and second, the reliance upon legislative changes for a formalized, nationalist policing. Importantly, this work presents a new and contextualized analysis of the logics that inspire this form of nationalism, as well as the mechanisms through which it is used.

When compared to the nationalist policies of the Western empires—specifically the United States, France, Britain, Portugal, Spain, Belgium, and the Netherlands—the nations that are now struggling with this process do so with very different globalized contingencies. Whereas these powerful nations used certain territorial processes to secure their nationalist identities– securitization of borders, domestic segregation, and differentiating public from private concerns (Canaday 2009; Luibheid 2002; Somerville 2005)– the challenges of newer nations invert these migratory patterns. As demonstrated by the jurisdiction clause, international travel, emigration, return migration, and the cultural changes that occur when righteous peoples enter foreign lands become challenges unique to this postcolonial context. For these reasons, we see the Anti-Homosexuality Act procuring "comprehensive" territorial measures: it demands homosexual Ugandan expatriates to return to be tried and imprisoned.

The legislation also exposes anxiety regarding the ways in which technology undermines spatial boundaries. The wording of the Principle, as well as within the Act and within debate, stresses the damage caused by exposure to "uncensored information technologies." As the Anti-Pornography Bill became an Act the day before the AHA, a thorough attempt to limit the spread of technology that promotes homosexuality can be witnessed.

Whereas much of the literature on sexuality and citizenship has thus far focused on contemporary Western processes, this work has focused on the legislative development with a postcolonial context that has much to contribute. Therefore, what is largely understood about the geography of sexual citizenship is the way in which the increased presence of foreign peoples—through immigration—changes the legislative landscape of a nation and exposes national anxieties around race, sexuality, and gender. This research shows how postcolonial conditions change this nationalist understanding and experience. Information technologies, foreign organizational bodies, economic vulnerability, and international exposure are blamed for moral degradation. The infiltration in this circumstance is not the presence of alien peoples, but the implantation of alien ideology into vulnerable, native peoples. Accordingly, this legislation advanced in order to address these simultaneous processes. It holds analytical value regardless of whether or not it ever becomes or remains law.

Thirty-eight countries in Africa, alone, criminalize same sex sexual acts. Over half of the 79 countries across the world that currently criminalize sodomy do so as a result of British colonial law (Gupta 2008). As Great Britain did not decriminalize same sex relations until 1967, the anti-sodomy laws in countries that achieved independence from Britain before this process, such as Uganda in 1962, were unchanged. That is, the British enacted this law and enforced it on their colonies, and left with it intact. Therefore, Uganda becomes an important case: exemplary for the hyper-visible way through which it has experienced these changes, but comparable for its history with anti-sodomy legislation, its current concerns of cultural imperialism, and its effort to utilize homophobic nationalism in order for development. Understanding the ethno-racial and geo-social politics of sexual citizenship can help shed much needed light on the nations that currently debate similar legislative developments such as the Anti-Homosexuality Act.

NOTES

1. An earlier version of Chapter 1 appears in the journal, *Comparative Sociology*, volume 16, issue 3.
2. The Anti-Homosexuality Act, as passed, defined the offense of homosexuality as touching or penetrating a person of the same sex with any body part or sexual contraption. Aggravated homosexuality can occur through several crimes, including repeat offenses; same sex pedophilia; same sex parent-child incest; living with HIV; administering a drug to enable sex; or the "victim" has a disability.
3. *Kuchu* is a term used by Ugandans that encompasses each SGL and GNC identity. It was popularized in the late 2000s by activists of Sexual Minorities Uganda (SMUG).
4. In July 2009, through the efforts of the Indian NGO the Naz Foundation, India revised the Penal Code to exclude homosexual consensual sex between adults from Section 377. However, in 2013, the Indian Supreme Court struck down the revision, choosing to uphold Section 377.
5. Jordan cites Peter Damian *Liber Gomorrhianus* (Reindel 1:287.19–21) and refers to the text as Liber throughout his notes.

6. Two other instances of penalty for male-male sex are known, both with different (arguably irrelevant) stipulations: the Roman Republic penalized adult male sex with male minors when the minor was not a prostitute or slave; and the Middle Assyrian Code criminalized sex between comrades in the military (Code of Assura, as copied by J.S. Arkenberg; Boswell 1980).

7. Indirect rule was the system that the British used to regulate the colonies with low levels of settlement. They set up agencies for "Native Affairs"; appointed certain people to positions of leadership, such as judges to enforce the Penal Code or Customary Law; and largely contracted labor from afar.

8. Epprecht notes that between 1892–1923, 90 percent of the 300 cases of sodomy that came before the white magistrates in Rhodesia involved sex between native Africans.

9. November 6, 2003; Hansard Parliamentary Report.

10. December 20, 2013; Hansard Parliamentary Report.

11. November 6, 2003; Hansard Parliamentary Report.

12. December 15, 2009; Hansard Parliamentary Report.

Chapter Two

Invisibility Matters

Visibility Management in a Transnational Age

It is clear from the parliamentary text, news outlets,[1] and the self-reported founding dates of kuchu organizations that sexual justice organizing existed and thrived long before the Anti-Homosexuality Bill and international attention. Anglican priest Rev. Erich Kasirye founded an outreach group for gay (then referred to as "homosexual") people in 1999, which had a mission to provide spiritual and emotional support for LGBT people.[2] In 2001, alongside Bishop Christopher Ssenyonjo, the group formed transnational ties with Integrity USA, a nonprofit organization working for full inclusion into the rites and community of the Episcopal Church. In that year, it became an international affiliate of the organization, called *Integrity Uganda.* Gay and Lesbian Alliance (GALA) Uganda also formed in 2001, with the broad goal to improve the "emotional, social, political, educational, and spiritual lives of LGBT Ugandans."[3] Although Integrity Uganda was not an organization founded *by* LGBT people, it reportedly transitioned into gay leadership by 2003 while retaining strong connections to straight allies within the faith community (Senteza 2003). The previous chapter mentioned Integrity Uganda, as it was the first LGBT organization discussed by parliament and by the Ugandan government-founded newspaper, *The New Vision,* for attempting to seek international funding.

In the same year as Integrity Uganda's transition into gay leadership, Freedom and Roam Uganda (FARUG) developed as the first organization for lesbians.[4] Existing today with an expanded focus on lesbian, bisexual, transgender, intersex/queer people, FARUG has become the longest lasting kuchu group in Kampala. Founders of FARUG cite a lesbian-run bar called Dizzy Drop House as the epicenter of the nascent community of queer women and gender non-conforming people in the early 2000s (Minor 2014). By 2004, Sexual Minorities Uganda (SMUG) formed to provide community resources for all LGBTI and has since assumed the role of an umbrella organization, subsuming FARUG and ten other member organizations by 2018.

Many kuchu organizations have existed within and outside of this umbrella, achieving various levels of success with grassroots organizing, research, and reporting, or offering resources to community members. Within the decade from 200–013, the movement graduated (or, arguably, factionalized) from two to twenty NGOs for LGBTI rights (Minor 2014).

It is quite clear that at least a core group of kuchu activists had minted various organizational management practices before the AHB and AHA. However, during my time in Kampala, several kuchus over the age of 35 shared their belief that anti-gay hostilities had increased noticeably with the "new era of activism." They reminisced about the times when gays congregated at bars and private house parties without as much worry. However, scrutiny heightened in the mid-2000s, and increased even more sharply with the proposal of the AHB. Therefore, this chapter focuses on the visibility management strategies employed by activists at this time of heightened scrutiny.

The memory of a particular exchange rests in the forefront of my mind as I navigate these questions. Before I meet with Cherish, a transwoman who spearheaded an organization for trans empowerment, John tells me "That man will get us in trouble. He brings all the bad attention with his dressing and his fake woman-shit. You cannot meet that one here."[5] John is a bisexual, cisgender man and the person he was referring to, Cherish, is a feminine transwoman. We sat in his car, in front of his business, finishing an interview where he told me about his history organizing through entrepreneurial efforts and his political beliefs about the role LGBT people should play in their communities. Despite his statement's obvious and offensive transphobia, at the root of John's words is a concern for the type of visibility that his business would receive. The inclusion of trans* and gender non-conforming people (and bisexuals, for that matter) into movements for the rights and safety of lesbian and gay people, has been a challenge in many geographic contexts. Therefore, unlike my previous two meetings with kuchu organizers, where we had the safety of John and Isaac's walls or at least proximity to it, Cherish and I had to choose another setting to meet.

"Kensington Gardens and Golf"[6] I say to Samuel, who has become my trusted boda-boda (motorbike-taxi) driver.

"Ma'am?" he responds. I repeat it, to no avail. Samuel looks at me, puzzled, and I'm worried that he's having a hard time understanding my accent again.

"Which neighborhood?" he asks for clarification. It was the same neighborhood as I had visited the day before, so I asked him to just drop me where

I had met John and Isaac, with hopes that I would get more information from Cherish by the time we reached.

I tell him everything that Cherish told me, but honestly I'm worried that she hasn't given me a real meeting place. It's our third attempt at meeting up and she stood me up each time before. I don't understand why—if it is an organizational issue, or if she doesn't want to meet with me—but the last worry (and most present at the time) didn't quite make sense, since she had eagerly reached out for us to make a connection.

I had met Cherish in New York in October 2013, between my trips to Kampala. She attended an event that my organization hosted, where two Argentinian transmen shared with us their successful campaign for a national gender identity law. We spoke briefly and excitedly after the event, and I promised her I would look for her when I returned to Kampala.

After an hour of riding around (for what should have been a fifteen-minute commute) and of conversation about my accent, religion, and how I'm not yet engaged to be married, Samuel pointed into the distance *"maybe it's that!"* We saw a beautiful sign grounded in vast gardens that covered the hill. I asked him if he had ever seen the area before, *"no ma'am, it is beautiful but I've never noticed it. Perhaps it is for the Europeans?"*

I understand immediately what he means, but it strikes me that not one Ugandan person from whom I had asked directions had ever been to this place. It is large and beautiful and has an air that makes me think of The Plantation Inn, a country club where white people (the few middle class ones, at least) that I grew up with had often dined. They always responded incredulously when I had said that I hadn't been—hadn't seen it—didn't want to visit—wasn't interested.

It's curiously situated in a normal, non-tourist, working class residential area. Seemingly out of nowhere, there is this high investment commercial property, where people are celebrating a wedding and others are enjoying (relatively) high-priced meals.

Samuel tells me it is best, if I am only to stay for an hour or two, for him to stay in the area and for me to pay for his time and the ride home. I think this is good advice, since I look around and it is completely open. There are no boda stands around and walking back to the main road would take quite some time, only to have to get a driver from there. I count the amount of cash I have, to make sure that I would have a little left over if I agree. I'm leaving for New York the next day and am at the point of the trip when my funds have been measured to last for just the trip home and final meal.

I call Cherish when I'm at the entrance. Cherish lives nearby and had walked over when I had indicated that I was close. I join her at the bar in the front, where she was sitting with the beer she had ordered to justify being in this commercial space. It was clear however that she didn't intend on paying for it; a vibe that the server undoubtedly picked up on and looked relieved when I showed up. I let Cherish know that I actually didn't have enough shillings on me to buy her more than two drinks since I had to pay more than I had anticipated for the ride. She didn't intend on spending money, so I imagine it was assumed that I'd have enough.

We begin talking about various topics. Mostly, we focus on the history and future of her organization and what my intentions are for my writing. We also, in light of a conversation that I had with others about my desire to meet with her, broach the subject of coalition building. After a pause in the largely casual, honest, and relaxed conversation, I look at the picturesque sign on the hill; observe the wedding bustle; and eventually I catch the eyes of the server, who was watching us, more confused than hostile.

We, together, are visibly strange. We are exposed but likely illegible in this environment. Cherish is clearly trying to manage the visibility of her queerness—she's dressed "as a man" (her words), but she can't be read as manly. Her vibrancy, her sass, her sway, her effeminate gestures are giving her away. She's somewhere in between, in this moment, in this overwhelmingly cis-space and we both sit here, in a completely unreadable relationship.

I imagine the server's confusion. Why am I with her? Why is she acting this way/dressed this way? Why does she expect me to pay for her drink? Why don't I have enough money to drink myself? Or for us to eat? Why has she brought a laptop; me a notebook? We are clearly not a couple. There is an economic power dynamic that is likely obvious. We are comfortable enough to laugh together, but not close enough for any affection. We also don't look like an average pair of professionals: I look young and I'm underdressed in my blue jeans and simple t-shirt. She maybe smiles too much; is too sweet "for a man." There is an economic power dynamic that is obvious and inverted, as I am read as a woman (a reading that I do not identify with, but do acknowledge).

It's all queer and I'm hyperaware of our strangeness, as everyone stares. We're uncovered, unprotected, but our interactions are genuine and comfortable and it is clear that we share a likeness or familiarity. It occurs to me that this is the type of organizing experience that I value, the very beginning of a collaborative relationship. However, this is also a formation that is growing increasingly subjected to scrutiny by government and ordinary citizens like the server.

In this moment, the Anti-Homosexuality Bill has passed into an Act that has not yet been nullified. This is my second extended stay in Uganda and while I have the wherewithal to technically navigate the city, the straight gaze noticeably affected my navigation of several social situations. For one, as opposed to the previous year, I spent this 2014 trip almost entirely in the company of other queer people. My previous ethnographic aim had been to observe and socialize with straight and cisgender people, so as to get a sense of the heterosexual civilian responses to the government's interests. The queer experiences that I had in 2013 were per chance; the queer experiences in 2014 were by design. Perhaps more important than design, however, is the timing, as we had no idea at that point whether or not the law would stand or change.

It occurred to me as an obvious next-step, in that climate of anti-gay policing, to question the role of visibility, invisibility, and alliance-building as empowerment strategies of kuchu activists. Primarily in conversation with Ashley Currier's 2012 text, *Out in Africa,* this chapter examines these strategies and addresses two questions: *when do queer bodies choose to remain invisible?* Also, *how and why do allies violate that autonomy?* I use "bodies" to refer to both organizational structures—bodies of queer people—and to one's individual, physical body.

When do queer bodies choose to remain invisible?

The narrative of "coming out of the closet" relies on the assumption that visibility is a one-way street: a queer body exits the closet and enters into a realm of full transparency. Once one is out of the closet, one does not return willingly (if ever). This transparency leads to representation, and representation leads to progress. However, imagining this as a clean trajectory is a fallacy. A full understanding of queer visibility includes the whens, hows, and whys of staying hidden, especially after the initial announcement of public existence. For example, Currier, a sociologist who studies LGBTQ activism in South Africa and Namibia, states that visibility decisions include both the management of visibility and invisibility as organizing tools for queer empowerment. A group may use "simultaneous strategies of visibility and invisibility when it wants to work with certain organizations in coalitions, for instance, but not be publicly visible to everyone" (Currier 2012). African queer groups choose select visibility in order to opt into alliances, yet they also need to choose public invisibility in order to sustain in openly hostile contexts.

Invisibility offers us a modicum of safety. It allows for a strategic determination of how to confront systemic power structures; which power structures to bother confronting; and when to do so. To live as African (or of African descent) *and* poor *and* queer is to live as activist, whether or not one is visibly protesting, organizing, or speaking publicly. We are constantly interacting with power structures that are here to end us. Navigating (in)visibility is a strategy that queers become fluent in, often in our youth. This written articulation of the importance of strategic invisibility matters especially for kuchu Ugandans, as they, for obvious reasons, battle involuntary exposure as well as the state—or interpersonal violence that often occurs in response to their presence in public.

I adapt Currier's term *strategic invisibility* to refer to a range of actions. On a personal level, actions such as wearing gender-conforming clothing or speaking in the tonality assumed of the gender that people think you are can encompass strategic invisibility. This looks like me wearing a long, modest skirt in Kampala, an article of clothing I never wore before. It also looks like Cherish wearing "men's" clothing in public. This is not to imply successfully passing: at times, queerness is suspected and there is nothing that dressing cis* can do to protect someone. However, this would all fold into strategies of *interpersonal invisibility. Interpersonal invisibility* may look like lying, evading the truth, or having a cover story. Although many regard "lying" as unethical, it can be strategic and done for safety. In a potentially life-threatening situation, when a parent or police officer asks about queer engagement, assuming an alternate identity is an important and useful tool.

Organizational invisibility encompasses clandestine practices engaged in often in the histories of many countries and in present-day Uganda. This includes hosting a meeting in private homes; using passcodes for entry or for sharing information; or occupying an unmarked building for organizational purposes. This strategy is key to the longevity of organizations in Kampala. Offices, for example, do not flaunt organizational names on the exterior and are often situated in residential areas. The "Gay Village" is located within a middle-class neighborhood of Kampala and is home to several organizations, despite what can be seen by the eye. Invisibility, in that way, does not mean nonexistent or not long-lasting. On the contrary, organizations such as FARUG that have thoughtfully maneuvered (in)visibility, have lasted with relatively few negative incidents upon their organization.

Lastly, *national invisibility* occurs when groupings of LGBTI people cease making large, public appearances intended for the country's attention. An organization may opt into national invisibility intermittently or indefinitely. Some organizations choose to go underground for a period in order to collectivize, plan, and reemerge stronger. For example, if an organization seeks to plan and execute a campaign, they may opt into invisibility during their efforts, and later into visibility for a march, rally, or press conference. Sexual Minorities Uganda (SMUG) successfully engaged in this in response to the police raid of Victor Mukasa's home, during the "Let Us Live in Peace" campaign of August 2007. At the close of the campaign in October 2007, SMUG released a statement that declared the following:

> During the press conference, some LGBTI people revealed their faces while others wore masks to represent the fact that anyone could be born homosexual or transgender. In fact, many LGBTI people took off their masks that evening and went home and sat with their families and friends to watch the evening news. We cooked your food that night, you ate it and nothing happened to you. We drove you around the following morning. We gave you a hug when you were so sad, and we were the ones there for you as a friend when you needed

> it. We cared for you when you were sick. You can see that we are part of the fabric that makes up this society.[7]

Activists opted into national *visibility* in order to disrupt the widely held belief that homosexuality is un-African, unnatural, or somehow unrelated to the wider Ugandan society. However, many maintained interpersonal invisibility throughout the action, by using masks and sitting "with their families and friends to watch the evening news." This strategic move provided safety for certain members, while disrupting the anti-gay nationalist imagination.

Other organizations may not value the notion that all nationals must know of its existence in order for it to exist. Otherwise said, widespread acknowledgment may be rejected as the most valuable source of legitimation. While a social movement strategy may be to integrate into the citizenry, and therefore push for widespread acceptance, another strategy may place more import on small communes. These organizations may have very targeted, localized campaigns or work entirely through networking. While organizational invisibility refers to the practices that constitute clandestine organizing, national invisibility is a response to the goals of the movement, which may rely on organizational invisibility for achievement.

The Anti-Homosexuality Bill had a strong influence on these visibility decisions, stifling the activists' ability to work publicly in Kampala. A clause called "The Promotion of Homosexuality," while never passed into law, continued to develop as a legal concept equally detrimental to kuchu visibility. Criminalizing the Promotion of Homosexuality is the Parliament of Uganda's attempt to ensure that no organization or individual teaches safe same-sex sexual engagement, financially supports a kuchu group, or enables open kuchus to live or work on private property.

While lawmakers formally withdrew the Promotion of Homosexuality clause, the Non-Governmental Organizations (NGO) Act passed in parliament in November 2015 developed and became law shortly after, in March 2016. The NGO Act recognizes that NGOs assist the government in providing "services like health, education and water" but offers that the existing law has a gap, through which "subversive activities" thrive (Memorandum, 2). Therefore, the Bill proposes to increase the government's ability to monitor and "dissolve" such organizing. It establishes a "District Non-Governmental Organizations Monitoring Committee (DNMC)" and a "Subcountry Non-Governmental Monitoring Committee (SNMC)" (3, c) and requires that each NGO register with the committees. The boards would "issue or revoke permits" (4, II, b); and "guide and monitor organizations in carrying out their activities" (4, II, d), among other responsibilities.

The NGO Bill gives the DNMC and SNMC disciplinary powers. Such powers include the ability to "summon and discipline organizations" through suspension, blacklisting, and "exposure of the affected organization to the public" (7, b, ii/iii/iv). This Bill also, notably, allows the DNMC or SNMC to restrict the employment of foreign nationals. Therefore, we see the continuation of many of the Principles and provisions of the unsuccessful AHB.

The NGO Bill is an attempt to manage the NGOization of gay rights. NGOization describes the rapid proliferation of professional organizations (Roy 2014), which coincided historically with the ushering of Ugandan markets into a neoliberal model in the 1990s. NGOization as it relates to homosexuality can be seen in the early 2000s, as these various LGBTI rights organizations began to form. According to the government, the professionalization of gay rights organizing is understood to promote the message that homosexuality and other "subversive activities" are natural, okay, or healthy. Although the Promotion of Homosexuality is no longer a functioning legal concept, organizers (kuchu and otherwise) understood the NGO Bill as an extremely invasive and limiting national effort. It consolidates what "Uganda" stands for and against by coordinating civil society in such a way that its focus may always complement that of the government.

Kuchu organizers know that the required registration of all organizations would push them to engage even more rigorously into clandestine actions. An organization, by the NGO Bill, is defined as a "private voluntary grouping of individuals or associations" and cannot legally operate without registration with the Board. Each organization must devolve information about the whereabouts of meetings and activities and its operations and purpose.

If an unregistered group is discovered in meeting, they are vulnerable to government scrutiny. If an organization meets or acts without a valid permit, it is liable, on conviction to a fine. There is also the possibility that, if this law is broken, the organization's director or officer serves a sentence not exceeding eight years in prison (VIII, 31(11), b). Therefore, the legislation criminalizes coordinated kuchu visibility; the Promotion of Homosexuality essentially passed in a more insidious way.

The NGO Act (2016) increases the government's surveillance and policing of organizing deemed contrary to the nation's goals. In this context, *organizational invisibility* becomes an absolute requirement for each grouping of activists, as this legislation extends past the criminalization of same-sex sexual acts and into kuchu organizing in its very essence.

The NGO Bill and John's actions serve the same purpose. They delineate who belongs and who is worthy of association. Importantly, they strengthen this process while under (imagined or real) threat. The NGO Bill forces groups and organizations that are deemed "beneficial to the nation" into visibility and those understood as harmful into obscurity. John's act of excluding Cherish renders transwomen invisible; it states the terms on which she can be incorporated into a public association. It is a similar violence occurring on different scales. However, the effect has a crucial intersection—which Cherish and I experienced as she navigated a clearly inauthentic masculinity in order for us to meet in a public space. Cherish's choice, to forego a trans experience for a potentially gay one is telling: in a place where effeminate men experience heightened tension, she still chose it over the peril of being read as a transwoman.

The visibility decisions of trans-feminine kuchus require an extended elaboration. However, what is made clear here is that when visibility and nationalist violence go hand-in-hand, transmisogyny problematizes coalition building. The possibilities for an alliance are diminished by the violence enacted on transwomen, when told that they must compromise their identity or expression in order to have a public, or visible, association. Although John spoke to me—and not to Cherish directly about having to meet in a disconnected location, Cherish knew exactly why she needed to choose Kensington Gardens, as opposed to one of the (admittedly very few) established kuchu locations.

How and why do allies violate the "invisibility" autonomy?

Despite the international silence surrounding the NGO Act, the AHB propelled Uganda to the forefront of global media. In the wake of the proposed legislation, even before its passage, transnational alliances formed both within Africa and between Uganda and Western nations. The campaigns of Western allies, in particular, have rested on two assumptions: 1) the known activists in Uganda need to be made more visible in order to garner material and political support from powerful elites and 2) the unknown LGBTI people of Uganda, who are suffering without profile or attention, need assistance.

The first assumption has proven particularly harmful in some cases. When prominent gay activist David Kato was murdered, Olive Minor was in Kampala. In her dissertation (2014), she reveals a strikingly relevant account:

> At the funeral, cameras swept across the crowd of mourners, taking in the large cohort of LGBTI activists and friends, the majority of whom wore black t-shirts with a photograph of David on the front, a rainbow on the sleeve, and the words "Aluta Continua" in white script on the back. Only Joanna—a minor celebrity in Uganda, who privately identified as lesbian—had foreseen the media presence, and wore large sunglasses and a headscarf in order to obscure her face. *What Rolling Stone had failed to do over the course of a year, CNN, BBC, and other outlets managed to obliviously achieve in one long, panning shot: they outed the bulk of Uganda's LGBTI activist community* (p. 209, emphasis mine)

She progresses a narrative which uncovers the anxieties of kuchu organizers in the aftermath, who had not prepared physically or emotionally for the exposure. Western journalists capitalized on their mourning, following the activists into spaces that they had crafted organizational invisibility, snapping photos of them that adequately display "the emotion" and then leaving to head back to their respective European countries (p. 208–212).

These actions compromised their interpersonal invisibility as well. Once coworkers and family members became aware of the BBC and CNN segments, exposing them in their mourning, activists Eli and Jojo[8] lost their homes and the slight sense of safety that they had developed. This violation of autonomy also occurred when photographer Rachel Adams flew into Uganda to *capture* their first ever Pride event: Beach Pride 2012. In Adams' write up of the event that accompanies her photographs, she quotes a worried activist who warned:

> You've got to understand that these people will say yes, take my photo, but they don't realise what will happen afterwards, the pictures will be all over the web and they're not even out to their families. We've had problems before with journalists coming over, saying they're going to write a story and then they just publish what they want. You have to get people's permission, and you have to understand that these people's lives are in danger.[9]

Despite the protestations of kuchu organizers about nonconsensual photography, Adams determinedly kept her camera. On this incidence, Minor brilliantly asserts that "anyone who attended Pride must already be 'out,' according to the logics of Western politics of visibility and identity"; therefore, Adams assumed consent (p. 225). These events clearly demonstrate that suppositions about visibility and what it means to be *proud* or *activist* are at odds with the strategic movements adopted by Ugandan kuchus. In fact, despite even the learned positions prominent kuchus are heeded as anti-progressive and therefore, dismissible by Western allies.

The second form of allied campaigns revolve around provisions of urgent relief to LGBTI Ugandans (not necessarily kuchu organizers). Such campaigns have largely relied on fundraising and coordinating efforts to extract them from the immediate hostilities faced. However, many of these campaigns have both fueled the cultural imperialism claims and frustrated the efforts of many kuchu activists. One such project was named "The New Underground Railroad," which began with the organizing efforts of American Quakers who call themselves the "Religious Society of Friends." They had reportedly "coordinated passage" out of Uganda for 107 kuchus as of 2014 (Schlanger 2014). The project received backlash both locally and on as widely-known of an outlet as Buzzfeed, which featured an extensive and balanced critique. The critique rested largely on the operability of the campaign. Neil Grungras, of the Organization for Refuge, Asylum, and Migration (ORAM), which works on LGBT refugee issues, told Buzzfeed, "In order to run a program like that successfully . . . you have to invest tremendous resources to understand the situation on the ground." Grungas also critiques this type of campaign for its difficulty responsibly allocating donor funds. However, even ORAM admitted to shutting down their own LGBT refuge project (Schlanger 2014).

Isaac tells me, as an indirect response to this phenomenon, "*You cannot evacuate a community that keeps being born.* These [projects that focus on getting gays out of Uganda] guzzle money and do not help."[10] His critique, although appreciative of international allies, is that it diverts funds from more sustainable, kuchu-led ideas. My critique is of how such evacuation attempts incite nationalist backlash. They reproduce an image of gay Ugandans, that they do not want to be Ugandan; do not identify with the country. For these reasons, kuchu groups in Uganda try to minimize the number of campaigns dedicated to this effort, as well as the amount of visibility that each effort receives.

Regardless, many "Save Gay Ugandans" fundraisers popped up after the AHA to "help LGBT people escape Africa." The "Rescue Fund to Help LGBT People Escape Africa" raised $14,025 in one month and was one of three similar fundraisers.

The campaign description reads:

> Since the Red Pepper Tabloid outed 200 gays in the most widely read paper in Uganda, there are LGBT people cannot go home, nor walk on the streets—the threats have increased dramatically. The need for support is now tenfold of what I had originally anticipated. This fund has already sent money to help more than 15 people in hiding. Some have received money for safe houses, food, passports, transportation, and more . . . the requests at this time for help are overwhelming. ("Rescue Fund to Help LGBT People Escape Africa")

A very well-respected kuchu organizer, Oliver, tells me about the lack of accountability that these fundraisers have. He is in a leadership position of one of the oldest LGBTI rights organizations in Uganda and is dedicated to creating sustainable progress for kuchus. His organization has attempted to follow the numbers for how much the founder makes from these and cannot see where the money actually goes. The organization also questions whether or not kuchu Ugandans receive it and if so, who they are. He is used to having access to such details, as the organization positions itself to know most kuchus in the city and events that would lead one to seek refuge.

The person who initiates these fundraisers, on the other hand, publicly defends that she has contacts who are not affiliated with Oliver's organization, who are in desperate need. Her circumvention of the major kuchu organizations is, in her words, a way to make sure that they do not monopolize the resources. The obvious controversy remains. Neither she—who lives in the United States and is not Ugandan—nor those who have spearheaded the New Underground Railroad have heeded the advice of kuchu organizers in Uganda. They raise tremendous amounts of money to "rescue" kuchus and relocate them, rather than invest in the movements to create a sustainable living situation for LGBTI people in the country. These campaigns do not rely on clandestine fundraising or collectivizing methods, as they would if they received support from local organizations. Therefore, they actually rely on strategies of *visibility* that may ultimately harm those who wish to remain in the country.

There's a tough divide here. On one hand, the threat of violence becomes unbearably high, especially for those affiliated with the movement. Due to international alliances, kuchus are more publicly recognized. Locally, they're associated with the breakdown of national morality and pride, and are made vulnerable by this negative association. On the other hand, everyone that I've spoken with in the movement says that asylum in and of itself is not what the movement should be about; that the amount of funds dedicated to "evacuating" kuchus surmounts the amount of support that self-sustaining projects receive. I argue that this, of course, is because nationalist violence is more visible, more recognizable to Westerners than the globalized economic violence of colonialism's aftermath.

The common anti-gay sentiment shared around the continent, that "homosexuality is unAfrican" relies upon the belief that inherent in the kuchu identity is a *desire* to leave Uganda (or Africa) and live in proximity to white or European others. It is a truly nationalist argument that reverses the logic of refuge; centering desire as opposed to an imminent *need* to leave. It also doesn't take into account the shared national oppression in the world system: that the majority of even kuchu Ugandans experience limited access to Western countries.

I'm reminded of words that my friend Keza shared with me on attempting to travel abroad: "I couldn't even go to my cousin's wedding in the United States! They rejected my visa because I don't have children. I have a job, I have enough money to fly back, I have family there; still, they're afraid that we will all come to visit and never leave. Honestly, though, I'm not interested in your country." These words became especially significant in my notes when, not even six months later, Keza had been "outed" at her place of employment. With the rapidly spreading knowledge of her relationship with a woman, it was no longer safe for her to stay in Kampala. She left for a neighboring African nation before seeking residency in a European country.

Liberal American campaigns that raise money for Ugandans to move to other countries forget that long before the newest *de jure* travel ban, there was a *de facto* ban on issuing visas to travelers from most African countries. Additionally, even if received in the United States or a European nation, the chance of obtaining legal, protected status in the country is slim. Many kuchus have been sent back to Uganda in high profile (hypervisible) deportations after spending years attempting asylum in the U.K., Sweden, and Norway—countries considered "more liberal" and easier to access than the United States. These deportations typically follow courts that could not prove the queer sexuality or gender of the applicant along the white, Western, and homonormative understanding of queerness (Llewellyn 2016). Importantly, the courts also demonstrate a narrow imagining of the harm that LGBTQ people experience while criminalized and hyper-policed.

CONCLUSION

In the era of the Anti-Homosexuality Bill and Act, global attention to Uganda and local attention to kuchus both spiked. The nationalist vigilance of kuchu organizing leads to conflicting processes: kuchus desire invisibility in order to fortify communal strength and yet international communities create hyper-visible campaigns in order to amass global support for LGBTI Ugandans. While both rapid-response and self-sustaining projects urgently need support in this current political moment, many efforts for the former actually compromise or undermine the latter. This creates a problematic dynamic between kuchu activists and transnational allies. This conflict has no immediate resolution, yet it holds important revelations about assumptions of LGBTI progress that disregard the importance of invisibility and autonomy.

The theories of visibility developed by Currier's research on South African and Namibian queer organizing enables my exploration of various levels of strategic invisibility. Additionally, it helps us to reframe the idea of what a goal is in transnational, feminist organizing. We can witness that allies often define their own goals, based in cultural assumptions that do not acknowledge the needs or realities of those in the local contexts. Grounding an analysis of transnational campaign work in questions of strategic visibility helps us to examine the complications of allying through a shared identity (queer, "progressive," etc.) across different racial or economic contexts. The only way forward is through a decolonial praxis, in which an activist or academic acts through self-reflection, sustained dialogue, and critical, contextualized thought.

NOTES

1. *The New Vision* reporter Dennis Jjuuko, for example, reported on meeting with organizers from GALA Uganda in 2002 in the article "Counselors Disregard Inborn Homosexuality."

2. Lesbian and Gay Christian Movement (LGCM) Conference. Conference Address, Christopher Senteza, 2003.

3. Although there no longer exists a website, this terminology was accessed through their text. Human Rights Watch also has this language, in their 2007 list for LGBT International Resources.

4. There are various lesbian identities in Kampala. Lesbian man, for example, is a masculine-of-center lesbian. The "man" in lesbian man does not denote a male sex assignment, but rather that masculinity plays an important role in the gender performance and/or identity of the person.

5. Field Notes, Kampala, July 23, 2014.
6. Retelling generated from field notes, July 25, 2014. The names and places referenced here have been changed to protect the anonymity of involved parties.
7. SMUG Press Release, October 10, 2007.
8. These are pseudonyms chosen by Olive Minor.
9. This quote was accessed from Adams' professional website http://www.racheladamsphotography.com/2012/10/gay-pride-uganda/.
10. July 23, 2014.

Chapter Three

Access Granted

Mainstream Methods of Transnational Organizing

In its most basic contemporary formation, we can understand human rights as the ideal protections that human beings are granted, indiscriminate of their national identities. One problem with this ideal exists in the relative weakness of its enforcement mechanism. Unlike civil rights, which are granted and enforced by the nation state, human rights largely rely on international bodies of governance, treaties, and inter- or non-governmental policing.

In order to strengthen a global enforcement mechanism, the international bodies, such as the United Nations (UN), grant status or recognition to certain organizations seeking to spread and defend ideals of basic human needs and protections. Accordingly, these organizations bureaucratize and form institutionalized, transnational advocacy networks that rely on one another for status, recognition, and resources. The most powerful of these networks center around the United Nations.

These UN-centered transnational advocacy networks seek to defend human rights by 1) identifying global abuses; 2) enabling small, local organizations to become self-sustaining; and 3) reporting the state of global affairs to other well-resourced organizations; to more powerful governments; or to international bodies such as the UN. With the intention of running effectively and efficiently in a global arena, this network largely relies on NGOs and INGOs to centralize campaigns and broker coalitions (Keck and Sikkink 1998). Traditionally, organizations within this network focus on policy reform (Bennett 2005).

With this chapter, I question the structure and ideological implications of transnational advocacy. I distinguish two forms of transnational activism, using Bennett's (2005) generational model, in order to compare both the highly bureaucratic, UN-centered advocacy and the more creative, independent forms of transnational work. Secondly, I ask what roles identity and structure play in the make up and structure of US-based, transnational human rights advocacy. In answering these questions, I describe regimes of understanding that serve to naturalize and reinforce power differentials.

I define "cross-world work" as work that exists between the first and third world, or Core and Periphery, and I use this phrase interchangeably with transnational because its language is disruptive, while *transnational* is not. The word "transnational" allows us to forget the disparities in access and privilege that exist between the different groups of nations, although it simultaneously invokes the imagining that the referenced nations include at least one Core country. That is to say, *transnational* social movement analyses tend to include at least one Western nation. In fact, human rights advocacy itself currently operates in a hyper-stratified world system (Smith and Wiest 2005). The term "cross-world" serves to reinforce our awareness of our different positions of power in the world system, which is particularly central to this analysis.

Global interconnectedness, facilitated by advancing technology, has undermined the ability that distance and state boundaries have to determine the speed with which a message is transmitted (Warkentin and Mingst 2000). Our proclivity to the idea of transnational citizenship and world polity has only grown (Boli and Thomas 1997; Clark, Friedman, and Hochstetler 1998) and with this, a global civil society has been imagined (Wapner 1996). Therefore, we anticipate that ordinary "global" citizens, as well as NGOs invest in transnational advocacy. With this global push, we now understand that transnational protest and activism function through various forms (Bennett 2005; Smith and Wiest 2005), often facing any number of constraints by state actors.

Bennett (2005) breaks down these forms of transnational advocacy into two generations: the first generation, which focuses NGO work on single issues; and the second, which uses direct action protest to advocate for multiple issues. Following Donnelly (1986), I refer to the first "generation" as the international human rights regime. The regime legitimates and regularizes the norms and procedures that adhere to the Universal Declaration of Human Rights, while centralizing the standards it sets forth, as it holds self-selecting nations accountable.

The regime functions through brokered coalitions and bureaucratization—or formalized rules and decision-making procedures—in order to achieve leverage over individual governments. However, this regime generally "involve[s] people and organizations in structurally unequal positions" (Keck and Sikkink 1998, 121). In the second generation of transnational activism, organizers focus on diverse social justice agendas, emphasize mass support and communication networks, utilize technology, and are more personally involved (Bennett 2005).

As regime analysis can "at minimum be useful in organizing what we know, expanding our perspective, and helping us to avoid some standard analytic traps and pitfalls" (Donnelly 1986, p. 639), I wish to contribute to this field of social inquiry by interrogating the inequities of access to the transnational advocacy network. Primarily in dialogue with Bennett (2005), Keck and Sikkink (1998), and Smith and Wiest (2005), I posit that a critical examination of the two generations of transnational activism will provide a necessary, qualitative look at the pitfalls and possibilities of the international human rights regime.

By focusing its work externally, often exclusively on what transnational organizers commonly call the "Global South" (predominantly black and brown nations of the Caribbean, Latin America, Africa, and Asia), the LGBTI rights regime broadcasts the anti-homosexual racial other—the agents of the (black/brown) state and the anti-homosexual "majority" of the countries—while attempting to unite the homosexual minorities in the country with Western ideologies, identities (LGBTI), and methods of protest and work. The regime then penetrates every nation within the "Global South" with seemingly unlimited resources and yet support for limited issues and perspectives of justice.

This chapter draws primarily upon my consideration of nine particular interviews with affiliates of US-based, transnational organizations. All of the respondents referred to their work as "human rights advocacy." Using Bennett (2005) as a precedent, I consider my participants to fall into two blanket categories: first generation, operating through the formalized channels of the international human rights regime, and second generation, operating through interpersonal (as opposed to institutional) networks or mass communication.

Their work can also break down into smaller categories, which I group as type of organization. Joe, Tim, Lucas, and Diana all work for human rights organizations (HRO) with UN-status. Matt works exclusively for a transnational gay rights organization (GRO). David and Judy work together, for a progressive religious organization (PRO) that David spearheaded. Lucas and Lina both consider themselves activist-academics, and consult for GROs. Lina volunteers with a Ugandan trans-rights organization. Alice works independently and entirely online. Her advocacy work is often used by NGOs and government officials alike.

Despite various nationalities, six of these respondents self-identified ethnically as white; one identified as white/Jewish; and one identified explicitly and exclusively as Jewish. One respondent identified as African American. Seven identified as Lesbian, Gay, or Queer. Two identified as Straight. These identities came in response to my request for "demographic information" at the very end of the interview, and specifically for the (open ended) questions of ethnicity and sexual orientation. However, many respondents had already noted their ethnic identity or sexual orientation, during the interview itself. The racial demographics of the interviews are representative of this type of work: the vast majority of US-based transnational organizations with targeted campaigns in sub-Saharan Africa have little to no African representation on their payroll.

I specifically recruited participants who work on initiatives for sub-Saharan African LGBTI rights from localities within the United States. This specification inherently creates a pool of workers, based in the Core, who focus on issues within the Periphery, the most exploited nations in the world. The targeting proves particularly useful in a few regards: 1) I am able to interview people who work from, at the very least, a geographical position of privilege in relation to their constituencies; 2) there is a very low chance that my sample completely lacks awareness of any national power differential. Although not all of my participants know each other, they all know and have worked with the same circle of Ugandan activists, among many other overlapping figures within the human rights advocacy network.

As I'll show, my participants seem acutely aware of this stratification. Whereas to some degree, this cognizance permits self-awareness and criticism, it also permits the adoption of certain discourses that, at times, limit these critiques. By interrogating the roles of power and bureaucracy in US-based, transnational human rights advocacy, I can both critique the pitfalls and highlight the potential of cross-world work.

THE UN-CENTERED TRANSNATIONAL STRUCTURE

As they are all UN-centered, the first generation networks traverse highly bureaucratized routes; meaning that the ways these organizations operate are relatively set in stone. This bureaucracy, in turn, provides an extensive reach, or breadth of countries or issues for which the regime may effectively work. This is the access that connected my first generation participants to Ugandan activists. In regard to the regime, quality work is achieved through three steps: 1) receive a request for help from a local organization; 2) build the capacity of the organization to advocate on its own behalf; 3) amplify the local organization's "voice" by appealing to the UN, or using a small network of high power media channels.

Step One: Receiving a request for help

Each first generation respondent reported that they wait to *receive* a request for help from activists witnessing or experiencing human rights violations. This is the first step to beginning a relationship with a local activist or organization. The only slight deviation to the uniformity is that Diana cited that her first interaction with a "human rights defender" begins after her organization chooses to whom they would offer a prestigious award: "We give the award . . . with a dinner and we partner with a recipient of the award and his organization to help advance their goals." Otherwise, her organization's model is quite similar: they receive advice on how to engage or "partner" with the activists.

Partnership has become an interactional model imagined to allow for flexibility, negotiation, and longer-term engagement. Diana refers to it as what makes her organization stand out: "We give them the benefit of our partnership with the award. It's not just the money. The award is not really the money, because that's just a one-time, lump sum of money when they receive the award in November. What we really try to do different is the on-going support." On-going support, in this organization's case, is actually much longer than what I've heard from other participants. Their term of partnership is five years for the set of campaigns drawn out for the particular organization. This "partnership principle" as referred to by Thoreson (2014a), grew out of the critiques that the transnational LGBT advocacy structure featured the same forms of "paternalism and neocolonialism" seen in the transnational women's rights movements of the previous decade (p. 125).

This first step, therefore, helps the transnational organization to avoid the critique of Western imposition. As reception is passive, it sends the message that the resources (the organization's expertise, the United States government or United Nations) are here when, and only when, the local organization wants it. This discourse allows these organizations to describe themselves as receptive addressees, rather than addressers, and therefore avoid the argument that they are imposing.

> Diana: We need to interact with a lot of caution and carefully. Especially with what's going on in Uganda, a lot of the Western organizations and governments are like you're here telling me what to do and then trying to impose their culture. We don't want to do that, we don't want to and we can't in this situation.

> Matt: I think it's really important to us not to seem imperialistic, and the US government has such a bad reputation in so many places that we try not to [act similarly], or only use that when someone has said "will the US government do this?"

> Joe: We don't tend to take action that they [the local activists] don't believe is going to be helpful. So we only take advice from activists on the ground discussing with them where we can be helpful and where, sometimes, we would be harmful. In the case of LGBT rights, it can

> sometimes be more harmful than helpful, so we listen to what people say on the ground and try to develop our policies in accordance.

Each of the respondents who have worked within the first generation network—Matt, Joe, Diana, Lucas, and Tim—have all been wary of confirming the "Western imposition" idea that resistance thinkers and activists develop. Therefore, Diana says "It's really about establishing the relationship and a rights-based approach where we are guided by the community on the ground and we make sure whatever we do, we do for their efforts." After which, she explains that "it can be different: with one partner, it may make sense to just do capacity building; but we may realize that with another partner, it may be about going to the UN." In the various examples given by each of the first generation workers, partnership led to the next two steps.

Step Two: Capacity Building

The highly specific, structured conceptualization of *capacity building* is critical to this analysis, particularly as it is one that the first generation praises for flexibility. In one sense, capacity building involves technical assistance, like building a website or using particular software. Yet, in the larger sense, capacity building is the process of shaping smaller, local organizations to work in a manner recognizable to the regime. In Thoreson's (2014a) analysis of the International Gay and Lesbian Human Rights Commission, now called OutRight Action International, an interlocutor named Kilonzo explains the following about capacity building:

> [It's] how to organize, to even start off, get support, do a proposal, fundraise, how to document human rights. Sometimes it may require you to help people with documenting skills, or if there is a legal issue required, working with lawyers, advising with the various options, even the lawyers themselves having a particular strategy that is sensitive to LGBT issues. At a different level, groups may [need] to issue a press statement, or an alert, or different mechanisms to respond to media, so they may need you to even help them with drafting, putting the ideas together. (p. 125)

Similarly, in our interview, Matt describes this step as assisting in writing documentation in proper format. He tells me that they "pretty much just call that documentation work . . . like partnering with organizations to help them write shadow reports, or help them like document human rights violations in a way that . . . can be used for advocacy." Tim refers to capacity building as helping early organizers to form an effective strategic plan.

Interviewees who work or have worked within the transnational networks noted that they have a standardized way of advocating for justice. As the organizations work to intervene in the midst of various global crises, they largely have blanket strategies and formats to which they do minor tailoring. Joe says, "depending on the target of our advocacy, the form in which we're engaging, we tailor our documentation and reporting [but] a lot of our recommendations across the board tend to be similar." Although they framed their requests as "advice," they have limited ways through which they are empowered to help. Joe continues by elaborating that governments "need to document [abuses], take action, hold people accountable for acts of violence to develop a legal framework to deal with these things." His work, then, is to partner with activists from other countries to "leverage the power" of the United States so that they may "look at where the US can take a leadership role and try to enhance those pieces."

After these transnational organizations receive the call for help, funding, or assistance, they help local groups write shadow reports, or document human rights violations *in a way that . . . can be used for advocacy*" (Matt). The inflexibility of the organization's method of advocacy is obscured by this discursive practice: the organizations "help" activists write in a way that can be recognized and responded to in the few ways that the organization is enabled. Therefore, it is implied but generally not admitted that there is a standardized way to advocate for "global" justice. As Joe explained, the standardized recommendations allow the work to be efficient and ensure that the effect has been measured in a "similar" case.

Capacity building permits local activists and organizations, previously unrecognizable by the regime, to create readable documents and reports. Thoreson (2014a) explains that, with IGLHRC, activists were "most visible to brokers when they framed their work in terms that were cognizable to transnational NGOs" (p.130). This framing extended both to the self-identification of those leading the organization (as "gay" or "LGBT") and to the readily identifiable language of human rights, or what he referred to as a "human rights-based framework" (p. 131). Capacity building, in turn, makes the local organization more eligible for future funding. This practice ensures broad, global access, but arguably at the expense of locally relevant solutions (Petras and Veltmeyer 2001).

After those within the first generation network receive "advice" about what to do or not to do in the local context, they inform the requester on how to be productive. This aspect not only demonstrates that the human rights regime utilizes certain discourse to avoid the "imperialist" agenda, but that it is established and routinized in a way which only recognizes certain bureaucratic ways of organizing. Therefore, although the transnational human rights worker may rely on the local activist for information about what human rights abuses occur, why they occur, and when to intervene, the transnational worker is the only person qualified to take productive steps.

Step Three: Amplifying the voices of the "Global South"

Step three, which involves, in Joe's words, "amplifying 'voices' of the Global South," has many functions. The transnational worker becomes an important middleman. After the transnational worker builds the capacity of the local activist, s/he can use the organization's status to grant the local activist access to international bodies of governance or influential nations. Each respondent from the first generation network described this along the lines of amplifying local "voices."

This report-back style of transnational advocacy undoubtedly creates nationalist tensions. As local organizations request help from and write reports for American organizations, who may not be neatly connected to the government (as they are NGOs), but do represent nationalities while convening with the United Nations, they reify a dynamic of moral superiority/inferiority. The image of the state, according to Joe, need not be perfect in order to effectively influence other countries, because he believes the US could and should be a "beacon of human rights" and able to "set an example for other countries." They, therefore, play into the "watch-dog" status of US organizations, which creates hostility within the nations under scrutiny.

The appeal for the local organization to engage in this type of transnational work is often the promise of funding. This mainstream advocacy style, in fact, relies on an exchange of funds. It is the impetus for making contact with first generation networks and it is what the "capacity building" of the first generation requires. In order to build the capacity of an organization, a local organization must have the financial stability to have an office and an employee who can dedicate their time to being trained to do such work and then to actually do the work. Therefore, we see that although Joe and others present a linear model of how they structure advocacy work, which relies on having no original influence on who appeals to them, we know that many organizations request help because they want or need money. This is why the "Western imposition" argument still holds weight, despite the unwillingness of US-based foundations and organizations to acknowledge it.

"Amplifying voices" discourse further establishes the passive position of the international human rights regime. This step enables the transnational human rights worker to provide the global ear for local "voices" to be heard.

> Matt: Primarily, our work is to listen to other people in areas that they work and to lift up their voices and to bring the voices back to the US.

> Joe: I think there's always a desire for [his colleagues in DC] to hear [the issues] or for us to channel voices from the ground or to bring those voices.

We can envision that this relationship exists vertically. "Voices" exist on the "ground." The transnational human rights worker visits the ground, by travelling (not by settling or getting firsthand experience). Joe reminds me that they "don't work within Uganda . . . We don't have any international offices. The work that we do internationally is conducted through international travel and we work closely with international activists." Through the travel and conversation, the transnational worker gets an understanding of what human rights abuses occur. They then channel those voices upward to achieve high-leveled, legislative accountability. Joe later asserts that "We allow them to speak themselves to policymakers. We are conveners." The language reveals a very similar positioning to Thoreson's "brokers" within IGLHRC.

Particularly interesting, however, is how this third step also helps to boost the status of the transnational organization and worker.

> Joe: Their voice is unique; they represent the community and another country. They bring a different level of, or allow for a different level of engagement with different actors in Washington. So I think we find it mutually beneficial and it helps our common goals to give them a little bit of profile. It helps us with the work we're trying to do on their behalf.

This "mutually beneficial" practice has strikingly different benefits. First generation workers understand amplifying voices as a way to gain legitimacy both for their transnational organization and the local organization. However, this model can only sustain one body—the transnational organization—in the long run. The profile for the local organization is short-lived, as the transnational organization requires new, urgent "local" issues to address. Once the sensational nature of the case rests, the transnational organization searches for a new setting of unheard "voices." The profile of the transnational maintains, while the local is forgotten.

Importantly, the concept of "mutuality" or "partnership," perverts the idea of expertise within activism. Matt is a white American who had recently graduated from college. With no knowledge of organizing, he gets a full-time job to build the capacity of activists around the world. When noting that a particular Ugandan activist was able to temporarily work in the organization, he eagerly adds that he is "so happy we were able to pay and support her." She, in the early 2000s, co-founded and served on the board for two of the longest-lasting kuchu organizations in rapidly changing Kampala. Somehow, she is considered lucky for a "paid" internship within his organization. This inversion of expertise is a symptom of the hierarchical positionality that accompanies the cross-world divide of "developing" and "developed" nations. Rather than truly embracing a redistributive politic, the vertical relationship implied in "amplifying voices"—from ground, to middleman, to international body—reifies the power differential of the world system.

This step provides local activists with talk-time with influential Western outlets, which is in and of itself a costly endeavor. Joe's organization has funded at least three of Ben's trips (either to do a media appearance or to appear before the UN). The flight alone of each trip from Kampala to New York costs roughly $2,000—the price of housing in Kampala for an entire year. However, traveling remains a crucial (and coveted) way in which kuchu organizers tap into these networks. Thoreson (2014a) explains that "potential partners became visible by traveling in the same circles as brokers. The world of transnational LGBT human rights advocacy is growing, but is still powerfully shaped by tight-knit personal and professional relationships" (p. 131). As a critique of this, Branch remarks, "This ersatz civil society focuses on activities such as holding workshops, seminars, and conferences, and, of course, on networking itself, activities that reaffirm a discourse that asks questions and gives answers phrased in, and supplied by, international NGO jargon. Its own expansion becomes its objective, the means replace the ends, and networking becomes a self-evident justification for existence" (Branch 2011, p. 146).

Mainstream transnational advocacy uses this blanketed, three-step structure at the expense of alternative forms of organizing that may be more culturally relevant and more efficacious. It stifles the creativity that could arise from cross-cultural connections. Minor (2014) expands in the case of kuchu organizing, stating that "the overall effect of Uganda's NGO expansion is a civil society bereft of genuinely democratic or radical potential," which forms in direct response to the opportunity for inclusion into this transnational sphere (p. 170). For example, ever since Ben's organization began receiving funding from Joe's, it has worked solely on documentation and advocacy through litigation.

BUREAUCRACY AS A HINDRANCE TO TRANSNATIONAL EFFICACY

Second generation participants criticized the mainstream, bureaucratic advocacy structure as limiting the efficacy of transnational work:

> Alice: So that [purposely provoking an anti-gay tabloid, in order to turn the negative attention back on them] is a perfect example of a different level of advocacy: taking the risk, maybe not doing 110 percent "the right thing"; maybe not listening; but really feeling independently obliged to "out" these people.

Alice understands bureaucracy as often a hindrance to making a difference. She credits the stories that she writes, her sources and flexibility, to her independence from the human rights regime. Although she communicates with people who choose to ally themselves with the human rights regime, and although she recognizes the value and the necessity of the regime, she chooses to operate in a way that allows her a creative "license."

> Alice: You know [my work is] very independent: there's no money behind it; it's not corporate. I'm not beholden to anyone and I do have a network in different arenas. I have my sources, which are grassroots people sometimes in the middle of nowhere that I'm connected to.

Alice has a professional relationship with activists all over sub-Saharan Africa and is very tied to her local politicians in California. She described to me several situations in which she was able to use the flexibility granted to her, to accomplish feats out of the hands of the regime. One such situations involved a lesbian UK asylum seeker who had nearly been sent back to a country whose main anti-gay figure threatened to imprison all LGBT people. Using a recording of a phone call from the notable anti-gay figure, Alice was able to use his words to stop the asylum seeker from being deported. In another situation, Alice was able to stop anti-gay "persecutors" from entering the United States, by convincing her local representative to talk to the secretary of state. Although the political structures do not grant her formal recognition or status, she can often use or threaten to use global media as a pressure tactic.

The mere connection to a wealth of local activists, or notable anti-gay figures in this case, is a feature of the second-generation networks. As opposed to maintaining brokered coalitions, such as the one Diana's organization has with one notable Ugandan organization, second-generation networks often gather mass support, or form coalitions with various networks. As she has diverse political goals, Alice builds a reputation with various, influential networks, from David Bahati, the author of the Anti-Homosexuality Bill, to universities across the world, to the "Executive Office of the United States," to "the government of Sweden" (Alice on the physical geographies of the IP addresses that visit her blog).

Through David's eyes, we can see the bureaucracy as reproducing a hegemonic image of power, and therefore limiting the reach that human rights defenders should have. David ultimately believed that the question that human rights workers should have in this area of Africa is "how can we empower un-empowered black men" so that they need not scapegoat women and sexual minorities. With this view, we can see the bureaucracy, which regenerates disconnected, racially privileged workers of the "Global North," and stops the human rights regime from asking tough questions that may lead to more effective answers.

The independence, or perhaps self-sustenance, of David's progressive religious organization allows a range of political campaigns in response to these questions. David's PRO focuses on economic development, investment, and theological reconciliation. Although it is an organization, and therefore has bureaucratic mechanisms, David understands that its peripheral status to the human rights regime, due to the religious and racial components, in fact makes it the most potentially effective.

There is a belief, by transnational advocates like Joe, that the bureaucratic mechanisms safeguard the regime against anti-imperial criticism. However, there is a counter-critique by those within (like Matt) and outside of the first generation (like Alice), that the bureaucracy impedes logistic creativity and emboldened steps to defending global human rights. Therefore, the receiving or "listening" discourse may create a more inviting image, but the first-generation network sacrifices the ability to actively pursue human rights abuses. The second-generation network often experiences the ability to "go with a more inductive approach" (Lina) and do what seems most effective or necessary. Therefore, those within the second-generation network utilize and access a variety of tactics, a flexible understanding of goals, and interpersonal resonance with the "target group" of advocacy.

RACIAL CHASMS AND CONNECTIONS IN TRANSNATIONAL ADVOCACY

Nearly all of the transnational advocates mentioned whiteness in our conversations. Transnational human rights workers, of either generation, often recognize whiteness in a context of access and agency. Privilege (typically) boosted their ability to learn a specific skill set, attend and graduate college, or move to the United States. This privilege, however, is not noted apologetically, but instead as a motivational factor or as a contributor to increased competency.

> Matt: I do find it conflicting that I'm this white guy working in this organization trying to achieve LGBT rights around the world, but I feel like I find peace in that because I feel like I'm more politically aware than most people and can identify these issues whereas some people would be like what I don't find any problem with this like it's fine.

> Judy: You know but there's still that internalized projection on to white people like we're the ones that get things done, and sometimes it's true. But, um, if it is true then I need to make sure I can use it to get things done in a positive way.

> Lina: the group that I will be involved with over there for HIV work, well it's funny because they're an MSM organization, but for practical reasons, it actually makes sense that *someone like me*[1] will be doing that

> kind of work because, well I just feel like that the hard skills that I have, they'll need because right now they don't have anyone available to dedicate time . . . like this full-time job of rolling out initiatives . . . that they're trying to do. I feel like in some ways that makes me more neutral, or more . . . or less . . . I don't know . . . maybe it's easier . . .like I'll be more effective . . . I don't know. [*emphasis mine*]

Although whiteness studies show us that, as a part of white privilege, white people are unlikely to acknowledge their race in their conceptualization of their selves and abilities, my respondents were generally straightforward about their perspectives on how their identities come into play. Matt experiences dissonance working with an all-white organization on "Global South," or black and brown people's issues, but nevertheless feels that his political awareness renders him qualified.

Whiteness, however, does not increase your access to interpersonal connections. Alice and David, in particular, envision themselves as inherently connected to the "voices" on the ground. As opposed to serving as a bridge, disconnected from both the bottom and top levels, second-generation activists often imagine themselves as embedded within the struggle.

David works with an African American faith-based organization that reconciles sexuality and Christianity. Joe's organization collaborated with David's PRO with the understanding that "if you can find other unlikely allies, those whose voices will resonate with the advocacy target. . . sometimes their voices can be more powerful than the US government or another sort of agent that we are working through or with." The demographics represented within Joe's organization, both as largely white and secular, reifies a divide that impedes the resonance of his message.

Joe understands his work as existing on a distinctly separate level from the advocacy target. On the other hand, David internalized this "voice," and understood his own as a part of it, not as a tool to use to amplify it. He says to me, "what would really happen if *our* prophetic voices, if *our* truth was ever allowed to be put on center stage?"

David's ideological connection to Africa complicates the modes of governing within the transnational human rights arena; therefore, Joe considered working with him "niche" work: a rare project of working with "unlikely allies." Transnational human rights organizations operate as a disconnected apparatus from the local scenes. The first generation not only premeditates the "Global North" and "Global South," or cross-world division, but also perpetuates it. Therefore, working with "unlikely allies," the allies who likely have the closest connection to the issues and sites that the transnational organizations work with, is nearly unheard of in the bureaucracy. For this reason, Joe considered his organization's partnership with a religious organization to be very special "niche" work that sets them apart from other organizations in the regime.

Alice, although not a person of color, connects her identity as an African woman to the various struggles within African countries. This connection integrates her identity and struggle with those for whom she works to advocate. She considers African issues "dear to [her] heart." Therefore, unlike the first-generation workers, who often referred to transnational work as an "opportunity" to travel, advance their careers, or use their privilege to help those who have little, she does this work because the issues reflect her own.

> Alice: I immigrated to the US and I was always charged with a little bit of guilt, leaving South Africa when I did (during apartheid). I've always had a strong sense of wanting to see justice and feeling very useless.
>
> It's a labor of love. There's no pay for it and of course it takes many hours of my time. I've never found a way to make it worth my while on a financial level, so getting the validation and seeing that it does help other people, I really appreciate.
>
> I've often thought *I need to become an NGO, I need to be salaried,* but then I stop dead in my tracks and I think *I don't want to become a fundraiser*.

This connection also motivates David, who understands whiteness as a potential hindrance to access within this work:

> They don't like the idea that I perceive, embrace, and push that there is a particular connection that African Americans have to Africa that is different than other Americans. They don't like that because it gives me a certain level of access that they get shut out from. White people aren't used to being shut out of anything. That's problematic for them.

David's coworker, Judy, tells me in her interview that she believes that being white is the reason why she should be a support person, as opposed to a leader; but also, why ultimately she should remain involved. She believed that her "white perspective," formed in the context of civil rights, is "fraught with pitfalls and landmines and all kinds of possibilities of making huge errors." She actively keeps in mind that her aim is not to be "some sort of colonialist missionary" but also recognizes that "there's no hope in clashing the interface around the cultures."

Overall, although most participants understand whiteness as a privilege, they also believe that it may become a pitfall in perspective. White privilege leads to an increased access of particular skills that complement the structure of the transnational human rights regime, but may also limit resonant frames, transformative strategies, or creative tactics for transnational movements.

I want to also consider whiteness structurally. White privilege grants my respondents access to this type of work, or to the qualifications deemed necessary to do this work. It provides these workers access to the status of a *transnational* worker, distinct from a "local" activist. Particularly in the first-generation network, the activists and organizations in the target sites are only ever considered "regional specialists" or "local" activists. Those from Kenya, working in the East African office of Tim's organization, are only permitted to work on East African issues. The same logic applies for Matt's organization (Diana and Joe's do not have offices or branches in the "Global South," they always work remotely).

With the international human rights regime, citizenship divides you into *transnational* advocate or *local* (Black/Brown) activist. We see this both in the sense of the increased opportunity structure that allows citizens of Core nations to enter this field (Smith and Wiest 2005) and in the discursive separations between "transnational" and "regional" from these interviews. As workers within this regime are over-represented in the white ethnic or racial category, we can, transitively, understand that whiteness increases your access to the "transnational" status. Arundhati Roy (2014) critiqued "the NGO-ization of Resistance" as organizational structures that "make the (dark) people of those (dark) countries seem like pathological victims. . .in need of the white man's help. They unwittingly reinforce racist stereotypes and reaffirm the achievements, the comforts and the compassion (the tough love) of Western civilization." In this divide, access is not the only confirmation of power. The labeling itself lends *expertise* to the transnational, but merely *experience* to the local.

The mainstream movement downplays the work and learned perspectives of queer-identified people of the diaspora. Take, for example, the interaction between Joe's and David's organizations. David works with an African American faith-based organization that seeks to reconcile sexuality and Christianity. Although the organization largely focuses on domestic issues, the transnational work focuses on this theological reconciliation alongside economic development and self-sustenance of Black LGBTI people around the world. David has worked with kuchu organizers on several occasions, both in the United States and in Uganda. His organization has invested in land for Ugandan LGBTI people to clear, farm, and live on.[2] It has worked through religious channels to empower Ugandan ministers who hope to combat anti-gay fervor as well as confronting anti-gay ministers in East Africa.

Joe's organization collaborated with David's, in result of a suggestion made by one kuchu organizer who considers himself very religious. Joe, however, regards religious organizations as a distinctly separate group from "leaders of human rights." In his words, this work shows the strength of his organization, which has created a "niche" out of working with those who typical, or larger human rights organizations would not work with.

> . . . the faith leaders is a good example of that [niche work]. The human rights community and faith leaders coming together for human rights. That's an example of where human rights and moderate faith leaders, we don't agree on a lot of things, but what we're trying to do is come to a consensus that violence and criminalization is antithetical to the human rights and to Christian values and we all need to speak out against it and promote change in Uganda and elsewhere.

Joe states that their organization has to carve out niches in order for their work to succeed, whereas larger groups such as Amnesty International don't have to bother to collaborate with organizations outside of their immediate coalitions. However, this collaboration strengthens their group and often makes their message "more resonant."

> Joe: If you can find other unlikely allies, those whose voices will resonate with the advocacy target, you know we may not agree with them on issues, but sometimes their voices can be more powerful than the US government or another sort of agent that we are working through or with.

There is obvious virtue in Joe's organization taking the leap to make this connection. However, on the other side, it is clear that this way of regarding David's organization relies on a presupposition that their faith-based work is marginal. David's organization is undersourced, or used and valued less than it logically should be. His perspective is sidelined by the mainstream groups, which see him as an "unlikely ally." I openly wonder how, if not for the erasure of black queer subjectivity, could David, a gay man of African descent, be an *unlikely* ally to work with LGBTI Africans?

In mainstream, US-based organizing, religion is almost always taken out of the equation and secular work is privileged. This is because whites (LGBTI people, human rights workers, etc.) in the United States are much more likely to reject religion than their black counterparts. While 48 percent of the general population of LGBT people say they have no religious affiliation; only 15 percent of black LGBT report similarly (or refused to respond).[3] Not understanding racial and cultural difference leads to the marginalization in which engagement with black organizations is considered sparingly; a way to carve out a "niche" in the otherwise uniform regime. It also supports Roy's analogy, that INGO workers are "the secular missionaries of the modern world" (2014).

Joe alludes to a fear of forming even temporary alliances with these groups: "there's always a fear that you're dancing with the devil or engaging with people that you have serious disagreements with on other issues. I guess there's some controversy and risk involved." Non-LGBTI Africans and LGBTI African Americans are similarly *othered* by mainstream organizing. LGBTI Africans are connected to the organizing, but only as "advocacy targets." In this conversation, the "we" that Joe uses is nearly always mainstream, human rights organizers. "Them" describes "advocacy targets," or Ugandan organizers, African American LGBT Christian leaders, anti-gay Christian leaders in Uganda, etc.

Perhaps this is why, through David's eyes, we can see the mainstream bureaucracy as reproducing a hegemonic image of power, and therefore limiting the reach that human rights defenders should have. David ultimately believes that the question that human rights workers should have while working in Africa is "how can we empower un-empowered black men so that they need not scapegoat women and sexual minorities." This line of questioning is radically different from that which generates the mainstream organizing. Although I would not agree that anti-gay persecution stems solely from "un-empowered black men," the framing provides an important alternative: empowering the disempowered, uplifting connection so as to combat the overarching oppressions should be the mission of transnational organizing.

Joe and "human rights leaders" work as a disconnected apparatus from the "advocacy target," as I discussed with the linear (and hierarchical) logic upon which the voices discourse relies. He believes *their* voices can be amplified by giving them time with powerful officials and organizations. David rejects this power structure and internalizes the voice. He understands his own as a part of it. Notice how the quote (previously delivered on the use of "our") ends:

> What would really happen if our prophetic voices, if our truth was ever allowed to be put on center stage? . . . They don't like the idea that I perceive, embrace, and push that there is a particular connection that African Americans have to Africa that is different than other Americans. They don't like that because it gives me a certain level of access that they get shut out from. White people aren't used to being shut out of anything. That's problematic for them.

The idea of "us" and "them" is an interesting one here. The "they" that David refers to are people within the transnational regime. Despite the fact that he, too, works transnationally, the whiteness of the regime distances him more from the work and perspectives than the geographical distance of the "target" site. David doesn't *other* the people he works with; he *is* the people he works with. Joe's organization does. Even Matt's organization, which is all LGBTI but also nearly all white, does.

> Matt: I think I'm lucky in our organization because we make it so clear that we're not saviors, we're not there to impart our expertise to help these poor people. We're there to help lift their voices and we understand

> that everyone can advocate for themselves, they just need a venue to do that.

Mainstream transnational human and LGBT rights organizations operate like this, a disconnected apparatus from the local target of advocacy. Race is an unavoidable dynamic leading to this divide, as many who identify with the African Diaspora imagine the needs of "us" and "we" inclusive of those within other nations; and yet, those of the LGBT Diaspora exclusively imagine "them" in the context of this work. That is to say, although a sexual identity may be shared between white LGBT organizers in the United States and African organizations with which they work, the sexual identity proves not to be the master status, or primary form of identification that shapes one's positionality and interactions. The Black identity does transcend the geopolitical divisions.

CONCLUSION

The "transnational" is imagined as a space created, occupied, and operated by white, Western advocates. Transnational advocates target "local" organizers in order to bolster their efforts, however, they fall into several traps. One of which, I hope to have shown, is inherent in this transnational-local divide itself. As these organizations often only target "the Global South," they perpetuate the very same savior complex that Matt decries; they rely on a racial, economic, and national disconnection that assumes that they have expertise and knowledge to impart. This follows alongside Lisa Duggan's overarching analysis of neoliberalism, as "issues, alliances and policies have shifted over time and across differing locales, but their overall impact has been the upward redistribution of resources and the reproduction of stark patterns of social inequality" (Duggan 2003, p. xiv). This transnational advocacy structure solidifies the disconnection and inequality by not actually redistributing the transnational resources: the salaries, official association, and majority of funds actually are recycled to the Western employee and organization in the Core.

The strategies employed by such organizations are equally disconnected from the target organizations in Uganda. In order to forge meaningful connections, such organizations would not need to simply employ people of African descent, but would need to reframe Black contribution not as an unlikely or marginal alliance, but as leadership in a struggle that directly affects them. Understanding a direct effect, however, relies on centering the actual sites of violence that kuchus and others within the African Diaspora experience: confronting extrajudicial police violence, familial isolation, and abuse, and street harassment would move to the forefront of the agenda, over or alongside the presence of unjust legislation. As I will develop in later chapters, the opportunity to realize relevant strategies is missed, as the mainstream US-based regime invisibilizes experiences of queer people of the African Diaspora.

Despite the obvious disconnect between US-based transnational organizations and their "local" Ugandan activists, kuchus continue to appeal to this type of transnational cooperation. This is largely in pursuit of the economic benefits that are afforded for working with the agendas of NGOs in the Core. The previous chapters have shown how the symbolic association between kuchus and these powerful Western institutions has led to challenging dynamics and setbacks in organizing. The following chapter, on the other hand, will demonstrate how integration into and support from this international political economy radically transforms the reality of organizing and movement unity in Kampala.

NOTES

1. I continued with asking Lina what she meant by someone like her and she replied that she is neither an African nor a man who has sex with men (MSM).
2. It feels important to note that although this investment was made, the campaign has yet to be successfully implemented due to a lack of ability to maintain full-time attention.
3. These numbers are drawn from the 2000 Black Pride Survey, "Say it Loud, I'm Black and I'm Proud" and the Pew Research Center's 2013 study "A Survey of LGBT Americans."

Chapter Four

The Economies of Queer Inclusion

In July 2015, the Supreme Court of the United States ruled that same-sex couples would be able to legally marry in all states. In the wake of that ruling and the waves of excitement by lesbian, gay, and bisexuals throughout the world, an image, recreating the "iconic Iwo Jima photograph" began to circulate the internet. In response, Fox News immediately hosted a segment heatedly discussing its creation as problematic.

For Fox News, this was a desecration of an important moment and symbol of American righteousness. For many advocates for social justice in the

Figure 4.1.

US, including the anti-war and anti-nuke activists of the Civil Rights Movement, this image symbolizes war and the dominance of American imperialism: taken within the same month that over 25,000 American and Japanese troops died; taken, shortly before the United States used atomic bombs to murder roughly 200,000 Japanese civilians. The radiation from those bombs still causes birth defects and cancers today.

The reproduction of this image with four, masculine, gender binary-conforming men with a rainbow flag, after the ruling of same-sex marriage, leaves a bitter taste in my mouth for a very different reason than the patriotic, Republican broadcasters. For one reason, this photograph accompanies the re-realization that the mainstream gay rights movement has produced a white, gay corpus that has no regard for the intersections through which American activists before have organized, including the transgender and gender non-conforming (GNC) people of color who began the Stonewall riot that sparked the gay rights movement. It also, interestingly, reminded me of a very real event that I had noted the year before: Neal Gottlieb, an organic ice cream shop owner in Marin County, one of the richest counties in the United States, traveled to Uganda to mount a flag in Margherita peak. He declared to President Museveni, in a note, "Your country's highest point is no longer its soil, its snow or a summit marker, but rather a gay pride flag waving brilliantly. . ." Later, in the same letter, he stated the following:

> In a country that is dependent on the United States to fund the majority of its HIV/AIDS care, where less than 5 percent of those with cancer have access to treatment and where those with access to electricity are still a small minority of the populace, does it make any sense to devote precious and limited resources to imprison those who should be free?

Gottlieb's exposition interweaves important signifiers of homonationalism, providing a perfect entry point into this analysis. First, those most privileged within a nation perpetuate homonationalism, as their capital provides access to not only travel when and where desired, as middle and upper class Americans, but to also unapologetically and apathetically remind others of their relative poverty and reinforce dependency as the more dominant nation sees fit. Second, these nationals uphold American exceptionalism in "gay rights" claims, as the United States only overturned its own federal sodomy legislation in 2003. In order to do this, there has to be a thorough dehistoricization of both American and world history.

Gottlieb's entire demonstration rested on the premise that Uganda should not attempt to imprison "those who should be free"—not realizing that the life imprisonment penalty that he protests against was enacted in 1990, twenty-four years before the Anti-Homosexuality Act (as explained in Chapter 1). The extension of anti-sodomy legislation to life imprisonment went, without much outcry by Americans at that point, because the nascent homonationalist political paradigm had not yet been adopted. Third, homonationalism upkeeps righteous, American imperialism, thereby entitling a man to stake a flag, literally occupying Ugandan land. His statement, that his arrival marks the day that Uganda cannot even claim that anything Ugandan was the height of the nation, symbolically marks the neocolonial repertoire upon which homonationalism builds. He adds in a simple statement, that "if you don't like said flag on your highest peak, I urge you to climb up and take it down," knowing that his privileges (as a white American, rich, able-bodied man) would provide impunity, even as he flies halfway across the world to declare gay identities as belonging in a land that he'd likely never visit otherwise.

This chapter will elucidate how homonationalism and transnational advocacy alter local dynamics of sexual justice organizing. A new, local economy is created when Ugandan organizers integrate themselves into the US-based transnational advocacy structure. This economy is a microstructure created by four national and international level steps: First, Core states create a global, gay superstructure that demarcates "progressive" societies from "primitive" societies. Second, the US-based transnational advocacy structure embeds itself in the superstructure, as they enact "watchdog" methods, working with primarily black and brown nations of "the Global South," rather than the vast criminalization and human rights abuses created by and enacted upon their own nations. Then local activists, in various peripheral nations, apply to fit within the transnational structure in order to gain funding.

This chapter's analysis relies upon several qualitative methodologies: interviews with transnational human rights workers and Ugandan activists across 15 organizations, and an engaged ethnography between 2001–2014 in Kampala, Uganda, and New York City. "Western" homonationalism forces a narrow definition of what it means to be LGBT through transnational advocacy with impoverished nations. Adherence to that taxonomy becomes a currency for which "help" may be exchanged. The nascent movement deforms as kuchu Ugandans fight for the attention of US funders and organize according to these international standards.

HOMONATIONALISM AND THE REGULATORY FUNCTION OF SEXUALITIES

Traditional nationalism relies on heterosexual coupling, as it has been imagined as the only relationship configuration capable of reproducing the nation. This idea of reproduction is first understood in the biological sense of populating the nation through family units. It is also understood in a conceptual or ideological sense, of reproducing nationalism—the identity of the nation. That is, when a heterosexual couple creates children, they teach the children how to serve the state. This service is meant to contribute to the economic constitution of the state via formal employment; or service in the military; or, if they are women, this service contributes to the private, domestic sphere by raising law-abiding children who intend on serving the state once they are of age.

Homonationalism, as developed by Jasbir Puar (2007), describes the process of normativizing homosexuality in a way that advances a nationalist agenda. This homosexuality, similar to the straight state, reproduces the established patterns of citizen service, production, and consumption. When granted various civil rights that centralize work ("discrimination") and taxpaying ("marriage") to homosexual nationals, the citizen is able to complement the straight state, rather than contradict it (Puar 2007). Therefore, as the perception of this population grows as an international market (Chasin 2000; Oliveira 2014) and as a diaspora or imagined global community (Puar 1998; White 2013), it increasingly becomes a state interest to integrate the population into state norms. This interest serves to boost the credibility of the state on both national and international scales, as citizens hold both their own and other nations accountable for gay rights. Therefore, by offering minimal rights and protections to homonormative citizens, the state stabilizes more of its citizenry and increases its leverage over weaker states. In its mainstream model, the gay rights movement fuels homonationalism.

Expanding the theories put forth by sexual citizenry scholars, Puar posits that homonationalism legitimizes dominant states with minimal risk to the state. The minimal risk arises from what Ana Cristina Santos (2013) refers to as the politics of containment. The state expands its boundaries "in order to accommodate and contain new subjects willing to be read as 'normal.'" In creating new boundaries of what may be considered respectable, the state "destabilizes power relations within previous oppressed groups" (Santos 2013). That is to say, by integrating a contingent of those formally othered by the standards of normative sexuality, the state contains—or lessens the reverberation of anti-state backlash from such groups. A powerful population of citizens (largely white, upper and middle class homosexuals) continues to expend resources on reconstituting the state, rather than revolting against it. The new "normal" pledge their allegiance to the state, defend its good intentions, and hold others accountable to match the standards. Meanwhile, they exclude those who are not satisfied with the new boundaries.

The United States and other Core countries capitalize on this form of nationalism by strategically deploying the "gay rights" discourse to retain and leverage power over Peripheral nations. Puar juxtaposes the liberal events of gay rights victories in the early 2000s (i.e., the federal overturn of sodomy legislation in 2003) with what she refers to as simultaneous conservative imperial conquests (i.e., the 2003 US invasion of Iraq). Extending Puar's analysis, Nichols (2012) theorizes that "queerness" as a dispositive has a dominant, strategic imperial function to separate and hierarchize national moralities (and therefore nationalities). Sircar and Jain (2012) add that homonationalism divides "Western progress and Eastern primitivity, where constitutional/legal protection of LGBTI rights serves as the marker of how evolved a postcolonial democracy is" (p. 5). This hierarchizing permits the neoimperial powers to appear as beacons of human rights, which then retains (or amplifies) their political leverage. They gain international support even in times of intensified imperial efforts.

In this vein, consider the following interaction. I attended a protest in New York City, in 2014, against the Anti-Homosexuality Act. The protest has a relatively small (~30 people), mixed (sexuality, nationality, and race) crowd. A white, gay man approached me, interested in my sign, which read "Uganda: Why Continue What Colonizers Began?" He befriends me on Facebook that night, and months later I see the following interaction occur between him and his white, female friend, on his page:

ARTICLE HEADLINE: One priest faces prison for refusing to hate
SUBHEADER: Rev. Christopher Senyonjo faces seven years in prison for embracing the LGBT community in Uganda. [ONE "LIKE"]
COMMENTS
FRIEND OF PROTESTOR: I've said it before and I'll say it again. We should offer sanctuary to any LGBT folk and their allies from Uganda and Nigeria, and then just glass the countries.
PROTESTOR: What do you mean, put them under glass?
FRIEND OF PROTESTOR: I didn't say put them under glass. I said glass them. It's a term for what happens when you nuke a desert—so hot it turns the sand into glass.
PROTESTOR: haha. ouch. [ONE "LIKE"]

This is how homonationalism delineates the "civilized" from the "savage." Adherence to or belief in the gay right of happiness and personal and communal affirmation demarcates those who deserve life from those who deserve death. The invocation of death by nuclear weaponry here chillingly ties into the Iwo Jima replication.

This demarcation affects community relations, both between straight and kuchu Ugandans and between kuchu activist groups, as they compete for the attention of the empowered agents of "the West." To continue, figuratively, with the situation that the woman advocates for here on Facebook, if a select few will be saved from nuclear devastation it becomes increasingly important to heighten one's (or one group's) visibility, choose alliances strategically, and distinguish oneself as worthy. These, I argue, are exactly what occur in Uganda in the wake of homonationalism—to the detriment of the sexual justice movement.

Homonationalism, as a political paradigm, allows nations and US nationals to demarcate "progressive" from "backwards/uncivilized" nations on the basis of "gay rights" legislation. As attention to Uganda's gay rights increases, I find an economy emerges. Activists begin to appeal to the US for funding, a process that changes the strategies of the movement, the alliances that are built, and the communal relations. This talk will focus specifically on the alliance building. I argue that, as homonationalism strengthens in the US, the movement for sexual justice weakens in Uganda: lawmakers push for harsher laws; Ugandan nationals disown kuchus; and kuchus vie for financial and administrative connections, as opposed to unified political coalitions.

THE POLITICS OF TRICKLE-DOWN PHILANTHROPY

"What is the goal of your organization," I begin my interview with Oliver, a self-identified queer transman, in the seat opposite of his desk. The office for his organization is clearly converted from what was once a house, the four former bedrooms now serving as individual offices for the employed activists. This meeting already feels remarkably different from the one conducted with Jessie, an activist who affiliated with an organization for "female-bodied" kuchu Ugandans (lesbians, bisexual women, and transmen). I'm comfortable in the cushioned seat, a comfort that starkly contrasts the feeling I had while meeting with Jessie in a dusty alley, sitting on a concrete block. A comfort that is increasingly uncomfortable.

"Our organization focuses on litigation, advocacy, and documentation of hate violence," Oliver recites. Although we had talked in depth in a more casual setting about what queer organizing *should* look like, Oliver's answer is telling: he knew exactly how to phrase his work when "on the record" with me, and the recitation is not remotely similar to an earlier conversation of ours, in which he spoke about economic empowerment of his people, self-sustenance, peaceful coexistence with the larger community, and reconciliation with family and spirit.

Oliver's organization is one of the oldest for LGBTI advocacy in Kampala and, unlike most others, has had success partnering with American foundations. Although at least five kuchu organizations have now existed in Uganda for over a decade, the Anti-Homosexuality Bill and Act allowed for substantial increase in attention from American foundations. The influx of financial support created avenues for organizing that were not sustainable earlier. Primarily, as the attention was called to the legislation, the financial support was intended for combatting legislative violence.

The organization, however, was originally created for a more comprehensive betterment of kuchu lives. However, as explained in the previous chapter, the formalized transnational advocacy networks seek to defend human rights by 1) identifying global abuses; 2) enabling small, "local" organizations to recognize and advocate on behalf of these issues; and 3) reporting the state of global affairs to either more powerful governments, or to international bodies such as the UN. The transnational structure features "NGO-centered, single-issue policy networks, that run centrally organized campaigns, based on brokered coalitions, aimed mainly at extracting policy reforms from institutional targets" (see Bennett 2005 on Keck and Sikkink 1998). Therefore, in order to apply to or potentially access funding, first an organization must agree to shift its strategies, at least in part, to litigation, documentation and legal work.

Although many organizations do attempt this in hope for inclusion, not all organizations agree to change. The requirement to reimagine the goals of the organization to be competitive for INGO funding has led to divergent responses. For example, John and Isaac, the two bisexual men mentioned in Chapter 2, began organizing fifteen years before the Anti-Homosexuality Act. After structuring the organization according to community needs, they refuse to focus their efforts just to seek US-based funding. Their organization is designed to "improve the lives of and increase the visibility of bisexuals in Uganda"[1] through community-based initiatives. Their anxieties about US funding were manifold, but one in particular, which I consider a movement deformation, was that funding is predicated on a shift from the original community-based approach to a legal approach that is newly considered "necessary." This approach, they believe, relies on a separatist visibility and a different type of identity, as the new allies of funded organizations have little to no knowledge of or care for Ugandan issues.

John and Isaac powerfully communicated a desire for self-sufficiency from the new structures. The organization they build with is another of the longest standing in Kampala, but unlike Oliver's, it has never been funded by a non-African organization. Although it has admittedly gone through several transformations, the goal of their work is, and has always been, to provide services for Ugandans. They have had several business startup ideas: a carwash, mobile advertising (men atop trucks who dance, common in some Caribbean and African countries), the internet café. They said that they would prefer to use foundational support "as Westerners use loans and credit," but that this system is largely unavailable to them.

As we ride from Nakasero to Muyenga, after the second unsuccessful attempt for me to meet with Cherish, a trans activist, John and Isaac share their perspectives of retaining religious faith, family, and business while also advocating for the LGBT community. Both John and Isaac are married, have several children, and identify as bisexual. The internet café that they co-run provides safe, unperturbed access to gay and bi men. The idea of beginning an internet café occurred to them several years before we met, and it opened in 2010. John's internet activity had been discovered, as he was looking at gay-related informational websites in the internet café they had used at the time. The manager, who cleaned the browser history and cookies after each use or day, had tracked the surfing to them, and kicked them out, at which point they were harassed and banned. John bribed the manager in order to escape assault.

The mission that guides the internet café is to provide internet to the entire community, to respect the privacy of the users. John and Isaac place this provision as one that serves the strategy of community-based activism: "when kuchus provide for the larger community, the larger community will accept kuchus," John says while driving. "That is the problem with this new generation, they want to be celebrities. They want to get American money and travel and be known, but they give nothing to Africans, not even us kuchus" Isaac adds.

John and Isaac critique Oliver's organization for the intangibility of its success. As Oliver's organization fights (and often wins) against legislative initiatives and the perceived legal impunity of homophobic officials, Oliver's organization and affiliated leaders increase in status. The benefits accumulate, as does the incentive to continue very narrowly focused work. Those who successfully appeal to cross-world networks become the most privileged. The most privileged are then most empowered to configure the movement, however they do so along the guidelines set by the transnational structure. This begs the question, who has the most say in the movement goals and activities?

For this reason, kuchu groups suffered severe factionalization in the height of the funding flow from the United States (between 2009–2014). Groups have formed to account for the diversity of issues within queer communities: trans advocacy, trans advocacy for HIV+ people, queer youth organizations, "WSW" organizations (that include transmen), an organization for bisexual men (which was created because bi-men felt that their needs were ignored and invalidated by gay men's and larger LGBTI organizations), sex workers only organizations, etc. In all, Oliver estimates around 30 kuchu organizations existed as of 2014, however, there is no way to account for the amount of activity from the majority of these organizations. Of the five active groups that I met with, four said that they receive no material or economic contributions from the "umbrella organizations" that Western donors support.

The Rise of Umbrella Organizations and the Career Queer

The transnational advocacy between participating INGOs (especially those based in the US and Western Europe) and Uganda's kuchu groups has created what could be understood as a trickle-down philanthropic structure. There is one umbrella organization for "LGBTI non-governmental community based networks" in Uganda. Smaller or newer organizations agree to be recognized as a part of this umbrella in order to be validated as official organizations (not briefcase) by INGOs and international funders.

In the alley with Jessie, Jessie's friend Shelly, and the occasional construction worker passing by, I asked what benefits they've found to signing on as members of the umbrella. He responded immediately, but without upset, *"none."* Then he paused and added "but when we apply for money, it is the only way they [funders] will believe that we are real."

Many foundation employees, but certainly not all, will admit that they have never been to Uganda. As the INGOs tend to work in partnership with several countries, they rely on funded organizations and affiliates and "trusted" kuchus to tell them who is and who is not legitimate, rather than witness the work firsthand or build relationships with new organizations. The problem with this, however, is that it stifles the ability of new organizations or individuals outside of the pre-arranged networks to organize. In Jessie's account, much of the ability to build a working relationship with those established organizations relies on mutual personal interests, skills, and ways of navigating shared identities.

The cumulative advantage—the increased likelihood that an organization that receives funding once will receive funding again—creates a financial privilege among kuchu organizations and organizers. This financial privilege most notably shifts the strategies of the recognizable organizations from community-based strategies to those determined by and beneficial to the umbrella organization, their funders, and the individual *career queer.* I refer to those who have created successful careers from queer activism by this term, a bit tongue-in-cheek, after one conversation with John and Isaac. Isaac says the new era of the movement relies on celebrities who believe "being famous is better than being courageous." He summarizes the post-AHA, and years immediately preceding its proposal, as an "elite enterprise" in which "mercenaries" aggressively ask for money to do work that ultimately separates them economically from the average Ugandan.

Career queers are a symptom of the non-profit industrial complex (NPIC). Andrea Smith (2001) argues that the NPIC redirects activist energies into career-based modes of organizing instead of mass-based organizing capable of actually transforming society. The NPIC encourages social movements to model themselves after capitalist structures, effectively halting any major critique of those structures. In this case, career queers are more likely to approach activism as a form of business; they are less likely to situate the activism in the perspective of a community, even if they argue that their activism is in and of itself *for* the community.

For example, highly visible career queers seek international media attention to gain the support of Western liberal allies in order to gain support for their organizations. This, however, is highly critiqued by grassroots organizers as they consider it detrimental to the safety of other Ugandan kuchus. Those, like Oliver, who receive funding and attention from US-based organizations can literally afford visibility. Although they are "outed" on international media, they are also afforded the financial resources for security. That is, they can place gates and fences around their homes, buy personal cars and hire drivers to shelter them while traveling. In addition to these financial resources, they also are afforded social resources that provide accountability. If they disappear overnight, there are rich and powerful allies to make noise, or if there is a threat against their lives, they have friends in the Netherlands, the US, England, etc., who can shelter them until the threat dies down. They seek the status increase for the hope of safety in the reality of omnipresent danger.

The decisions about visibility are therefore no longer a communal consideration, they are individualized; the individuals in charge are often the least representative of the economic realities of the community. Importantly, although the decisions are individualized, the effects are still very much communal: when a prominent kuchu speaks on a network, they speak on behalf of all kuchus—whether intentionally or not. When they come home, everyone associated with them is now assumed to be kuchu. As it is a relatively small community, this clearly compromises the safety of anyone in the network: people who attend parties or join in the shared social activities. It is in this way that the career queer, John and Isaac would argue, is as dangerous to kuchu progress as the anti-gay movement itself.

This sentiment echoes Jessie's early complaint. Of all the wealth that they suppose the career queer earns, the community sees none: little to no emergency relief, no opportunities for employment, no physical space provided for cultural or educational events. In my mind I question, as they speak, if even the career queer has anything to give them. Although they achieve fame: they are nominated for large awards; they make TV appearances; they meet "important" people, including presidents and prominent UN officials, I still wonder do their efforts pay off in terms of money and resources proportionate to the need in Kampala?

I'm left without doubting that whether or not the resources gained are enough, the image that this form of advocacy propagates is harming the intra-LGBT community. As unfunded organizations lose trust in the umbrella (and the career queer), cooperation between domestic organizations suffers. Transnational advocacy is once again seen as supportive of an alliance of the privileged (career queers and whites) and not as supportive of kuchu or African communities.

COMMUNITY RELATIONS: WHO IS WORTHY OF EXTRACTION?

The AHA put Uganda on the map for many Americans previously disinterested in the country. Initially proposing the death penalty for what was called "aggravated homosexuality," the new images of Ugandans as possibly gay made them relatable (worth saving, paying attention to, or supporting) in ways that they hadn't previously been for liberal US NGOs and citizens. For the first time, people saw empowering images of Ugandans who were trying to make a difference in their community in ways that gay Americans understood: they had a hard time in Christian churches, they fought unjust legislation, etc. Soon after the AHB, appeals to fundraising were made to transnational funders, INGOs, and other formalized avenues, and also showed up on informal pages such as Gofundme.

Homonationalism in transnational advocacy determines who is worthy of the "civilized" demarcation. As LGBT rights become the most pressing human rights in the eyes of the West, local queers have to make themselves visible to the international queer regime. They do this by integrating themselves into it; establishing organizational legitimacy and securing viable funding from the new opportunity structure led by the US. The attention and funding have adverse effects on the process of building alliances and recognizing opportunities for progress. It also concretizes LGBT identities in ways that are new and not necessarily applicable to East African contexts. Consider the following interaction:

In June 2013, I was in Kampala and hoping to meet with kuchus to get to know activists, artists: like-minded people with whom I could make community. After I had posted on the Facebook page of a local kuchu group, Kai private messaged me. They (the pronoun that I will continue to use for Kai) asked me if I want to meet them, telling me that they build with an organization serving HIV positive sex workers. They suggested that I come to the neighborhood they live in, a well-known slum in Kampala, and offered that I take photographs of them in the slum with their lover. This offer struck me as odd, as it was made casually and without reason that I could see. We instead agreed to meet at Makerere University.

Just before that time, a lesbian woman in the United States had ushered me to connect me with two boys—Peter and Simon—who had recently been discovered together in a sexual situation, by their parents. They were threatened, assaulted and kicked out. They were 17: too old to be orphans, too young to have any prospect of taking care of themselves. The woman in the US, who does her own independent advocacy with gay, lesbian and trans* Ugandans, had asked me to meet them to make sure that they were "the real deal"—as in, actually gay. As she had never been to Uganda herself, but works very hard to help kuchus secure asylum, she often had people "on the ground" in Uganda verify that those who had requested her help weren't simply pretending.

I wasn't sure how I would do this, as I would not police their intimacy, gender expression, or any other stereotypical indicator of their relationship/identities. However, I agreed to meet them.

On that first meeting, we shared a meal and conversation and I let them use my computer to Skype with her. I asked them if they had sought help with organizations in Uganda, to which they replied yes, but to no avail. I offered that we meet a couple of groups together on a different day, with hopes that maybe it would be more effective if they had a more privileged (older, educated) someone to accompany them. We met with one organization, which gave them some advice about how to begin the process of seeking asylum but swore they had nothing more than the information to offer. They ushered the boys to try one of the bigger kuchu organizations, but also warned us of the small chance of actually receiving material help. After this meeting, we met with Kai at a café at the university.

Kai brought along with them a friend and two European magazines in which photos of them had been published from a gay pride parade. Given the not quite friendly—but formal posture of the interaction, I wondered what expectations Kai had of me and what associations they had with my presence. I also wondered if it were so standard to "prove" or provide evidence for one's gayness in this material way.

Kai began to speak proudly about the organization that they had founded. In the small, empty cafeteria setting, Kai's voice strengthened. They waved around the first magazine with at least six pairs of eyes looking back and forth between Kai and the paper. "This was me last year at the gay pride parade" they begin, "you can flip through it if you'd like, the Europeans interviewed me and loved me. They put my picture here." Two pairs of eyes, those of my young companions, flooded with fear. Several others belonged to the employees of the university's café, whose initial incredulous looks (certainly a response to Kai's queer gender expression) quickly shifted into hostility. The round dining room seemingly provided acoustics for my next words "no, Kai, we don't need to see this here." Simon nervously flipped through a couple more pages before handing it back to Kai.

After an awkward moment of silence, Kai asked me if I had a questionnaire for them. I'm partially stupefied and Kai looks at me with an obvious annoyance growing. I had actually just posted about my interest in meeting up with people, getting to know SGL and GNC people in the city, so I'm wholly caught off guard by both the change in Kai's tone and voice, and then also by the expectation in and of itself. They continue, "this is usually easier if you have a questionnaire or if you've already come up with what you want to ask."

"I don't have anything pointed to ask you, Kai, this isn't an interview. I just wanted to meet and chat. . ."

Cutting me off and switching to Luganda to speak over me at the table, Kai asks their friend "why is she wasting our time? Doesn't she have money to give us?"

I continue. . . "I was also hoping you knew an org or two that could help Simon and Peter."

Kai looked at the boys and had a short exchange with them, in Luganda. . . Later, the boys tell me that Kai and companion did not offer any information, but instead needed to know for sure that they were gay. To my increasingly disappointed face, Peter tells me "they asked if we were together, if we had sex, if we wanted to have sex with them." He continues, "ma'am, they know they have HIV and they still want us to prove that we are gay, even if it means we will have it too."[2]

Mainstream organizing is so focused on helping Ugandans if and only if they are gay or lesbian that this too often becomes the centerpiece of conversation. Their ability to receive help revolves around their willingness to self-identify with these few words and present a sex/gender-discontinuity internationally recognized as queer, homosexual, or transgender. In exchange, people go through a number of safeguards to *ensure* that the people they are helping are LGBT, so much so that they often do not help others in need. Attention is diverted away from the national (and therein, queer) experience of extreme poverty and joblessness and is narrowed in on the ability to adopt and prove an identity created in the West, in ways that the West recognizes, such as Kai draped in a dress-sized rainbow flag, as shown in the magazine.

The transnational connection centers on financial alliances. The prospect of funding turned out to be the only reason Kai actively messaged me and (in hindsight) preempted that I would want to verify their poverty by visiting their home and photographing them in the slum. However, it is perhaps only in this transnational context (connecting with the United States, or Western nations) that this concoction of poverty, gender, and sexuality is so actively policed in order for someone to "deserve" support. In an age when asylum is granted for persecution based on sex or gender, and securing asylum under such terms is precarious at best, it strikes me that it's not coincidental that it is a similar process to seeking asylum: which is explored by scholars such as Cantú, Naples, and Vidal-Ortiz (2009), Luibheid (2002), and Somerville (2005).

The economy is a set of relations that foster competition, questions of worthiness. It is modeled after asylum and perpetuated by transnational human rights advocacy, as evidenced by Kai, who *assumes and pursues a very* particular relationship with a person from the United States who demonstrates interest in Ugandans. It's also not coincidental that when I was back in Kampala the following year, I heard that Kai had earned enough money "for their organization" for them to move to South Africa.

Briefcase Organizations

The economy created by this privileged, transnational connection also attracts the attention of opportunists. Oliver refers to them as "briefcase organizations": organizations created specifically to receive funding. These organizations are typically created by straight men that pose as LGBT, under the impression that kuchus get special attention by funders. In Kampala, it is widely believed that "whites give money to people who say that they are gay." As a consequence, straight men looking for a productive enterprise sometimes learn the language of respectable, recognizable homosexuality, and the language of the human rights mainstream. They then use this language to appeal to LGBT foundations and the smaller-scale fundraisers that have mushroomed since the AHA and syphon money from them. Many do not actually exist as organizations and create fake membership registries.

I meet with at least one such organization, in Bwaise, a large "slum" of Kampala. The organizers ran a slum tour as a cover business for the gay group they refer to as "Treasure" Uganda. I meet them with Peter and Simon, two boys who needed advice on leaving/seeking asylum. Their organization is housed in a tiny, windowless brick building, perhaps 15ft x 20ft, with a huge rainbow flag on one wall. There are two desks, each with its own boxy computer, and nothing else in terms of technology or decoration.

One of the organizers is in the room and notifies me that the other is currently on a tour with predominantly German tour-takers. He tells us that they go through the slum and allow Germans to take pictures of the people living in poverty, of the terrible water, of the sewage that flows in canals less than a foot deep through the neighborhood. The Germans pay for each tour, but more importantly, he says, they're paying for the gay organization to continue.

This is an (academically) interesting alternative to foundational support, I think, as I listen. I cringe a bit at the thought of German embrace of poverty-voyeurism in this context, but I have no negative or positive judgment of the organizers: where there is a demand, there is a person willing to supply. This is opportunistic capitalism in Kampala and in the world more generally.

The second organizer returns about 35 minutes into the meeting. Simon and Peter have already shared their stories and their hopes to flee Uganda and seek a "better" life in a (literally any) Western nation. The Treasure organizer receives this information and listens sympathetically. When the co-organizer returns, he poses for a few last pictures with the German tourists and tell them to "carefully" walk down one street to where their van awaits them.

The organizers then sit together and listen to Peter and Simon share their stories. I also offered my own, letting them know a few of my identities, experiences, as well as my reason for being in Uganda. They offer Peter and

Simon advice on getting a meeting with the American embassy, with concrete steps to securing conversation time with the official who was currently working there. They took the boys seriously in a way that I had noticed Kai did not, as well as the way that the boys had told me the major organizations also had not. When we left, they were grateful for the information although admittedly still disappointed in the lack of material help available.

When I recount the experience to Oliver, he responds with, "Treasure? You know those guys are not even kuchu. They are straight people and do this for money."

The economy of queer inclusion *creates jobs* out of queerness. As activism under the non-profit industrial complex veers more and more toward capitalist venture, adopting an LGBTQ identity in Uganda can be truly recognized as work. However, this does not actually differ from the system set in place internationally, as participants such as Joe (straight, white participant from Chapter 3) are also paid to advocate on behalf of LGBT people. The difference is that work is available for Americans who wish to work on "LGBT rights"; they have access to this form of employment regardless of whether or not they personally identify with the group. In the transnational model, the local activist must identify as LGBT. Therefore, "briefcase organizations" are merely one unintended consequence of this form of transnational collaboration.

CONCLUSION

As previously shown, the making of "celebrities" or career queers is indicative of homonationalism in transnational advocacy. INGOs create celebrities out of local activists by promoting their causes, personal lives, and image to the UN, in movies and documentaries, or popular media and publications. This promotion bolsters international support for local struggles, raises awareness of movements of countries that do not receive fully representative media attention, and increases acknowledgment for the importance of the INGO's own cause as defenders of human rights (see Joe's account in Chapter 3).

The strategies of local organizing undergo major shifts as a result of this international structure. The community-based model of improving lives for LGBT people, through employment, relief, political education, etc., transitions into higher-level advocacy that the community cannot immediately recognize or feel, such as litigation and documentation (Oliver's organization). The advocacy structure creates teleology of local organizational development, where the newest, least developed organizations (least recognized or funded) have a community-based or grassroots approach. In order to gain recognition and funding, the approach becomes more suitable to the advocacy level desired by transnational funding organizations (capacity building, documentation—which serve a statist, homonationalist organizational model). As the organization gains this funding, it gains recognition, which leads to a cumulative effect of earning funding: a cyclical relationship.

That cycle creates the career queer, the celebrity, and the belief that the funding given to the organization will trickle down to benefit the entire kuchu community. Madonna Thunder Hawk (c/o Andrea Smith 2001) observes how foundations only give money to well-established NGOs with "expertise." Thunder Hawk also warns that "these purported experts are generally not part of the communities they advocate for and hence do not contribute to building grassroots leadership, particularly in indigenous communities" (10). Thunder Hawk critiques a typical scene, in which an outsider (like myself) becomes regarded as an "expert" on the kuchu movement, although the expertise is a product of textbook and observational learning, as opposed to essential experience. Those with expertise should be embedded in the communities for which they advocate.

However, what does it mean to be part of the community in this case? Can career queers, who experience international travel, have their own apartments, security measures, personal drivers, be considered part of the kuchu community that they advocate for? Or does the experience of economic privilege belie their indigeneity? I don't have a personal answer for or opinion on this, but it occurs to me that this is the impetus leading homophobic nationals to disown queers as un-African. A similar resentment may also usher the critiques that Jonathan and Isaac delivered to me regarding celebrity kuchus.

Trickle-down philanthropy is symptomatic of what Incite! refers to as the *Non-Profit Industrial Complex (NPIC)*. The NPIC describes the transition that social movements made in the 20th and 21st centuries from mass-based organizing to formalized modes of employment. Incite! contributors argue that non-profit organizations, especially those with paid staff, risk losing their livelihoods if the underlying conditions that cause problems such as hunger are changed (2001). Therefore, it's not in the best interest of these INGOs to develop models of advocacy that lead to the self-sustenance of local organizations. Jessie, Oliver, John, and Isaac all, uniformly, substantiated this argument with their experiences receiving (or not receiving) funding. All complained about their unfulfilled desire to create a movement for kuchus that ultimately led to the economic autonomy of their community. Their funding statuses (never funded or continually supported) were indicative of their decisions to or not to change the goals of their respective organizations. But altogether, they wove a narrative that demonstrated self-sufficiency as easier to achieve before kuchus began collaborating with US-based foundations.

In conclusion, the transnational advocacy structure in place complicates local organizing in several ways. US-based funding diverts attention from initiatives that most comprehensively and sustainably help the kuchu community to initiatives that ensure that the Ugandan organization is competitive for US donor funding. This largely is seen in the case of the organization Oliver works with, where the earliest strategies of the organization included engaging and educating the community and providing relief for not only victims of hate and interpersonal violence, but also for those of systemic violence (such as starvation and homelessness). The changes in the organization's strategies have shifted gradually, but Oliver notes that they are not any closer to economic empowerment or cultural change for the "everyday kuchu." In turn, the lack of assistance for the community has led to factionalization, intra-group competition, and decision-making that is not rooted in communal needs. The economy also creates competition between groups for the scarce resources provided by transnational human rights funders and, perhaps most strikingly, requires a one-dimensional focus on what a movement needs in order to sustain itself or be successful.

Atop the strategic shifts experienced by the local movement are the insidious effects of including kuchus in the homonationalist project of US- and European-based funders. Those likely to be paraded as celebrities are those who most readily fit into narratives of the "appropriate" citizen. They fit into relatively rigid gender roles (tending toward masculinity, for cismen, ciswomen, and transmen). They can be imagined as the Ugandan corollary to the proper homosexual national of the United States. The career queer aspires to "work" for the movement, for the visibility of international queerness by any means necessary, even if it means allying with the people who would affect sanctions that immediately take away health care and food provisions from your country. It is to this message that the larger Ugandan citizenry responds. The introduction of homonationalism through transnational connections creates an economy out of queerness: that economy, in turn, increases the intra-group competition, decreases the cohesion of the community, and ultimately alters the goals of local movements.

NOTES

1. Interview, Kampala, Uganda, July 2014.
2. Field Notes, Kampala, Uganda, June 2013.

Chapter Five

Centering Afro-Diasporic Organizing for Transnational Futures

BLACK QUEER ERASURE

"Yes, I know what it is like for you Americans to come out, I have seen *Will and Grace*." Ben, a Ugandan LGBTI organizer, earnestly responds to my question.[1] Although asked rhetorically, I wondered aloud about the differences he imagines exist between our histories of telling our parents that we were gay and lesbian. The response catches me so off guard, so bewildered, that I have no words to tell him the truth of my experience. I am a Black, Caribbean lesbian living in the United States. I am also a community anti-violence organizer for queer people of color, working to end the constant hate and police violence experienced by queer Black and Latinx people in Brooklyn. We are heading to dinner and his demeanor tells me that he has largely written me off, as neither my organization nor I have any money to offer him or his. He instead skips forward to chat with a straight, white woman who works for the organization that funded his trip to the States.

The interaction leaves me feeling as though my existence is America's most closely guarded secret. It is in this context, a conversation held about "lesbianness" or "gayness," that my nationality has, for the first time, trumped my race or ethnicity. I am now an American, represented by Will and Grace, something I have never been before. This exchange compels me to question how lesbian, as a signifier, came to represent a lived experience that was never mine.

This erasure prevailed in the evening's interaction with Ben and spiked several times over the next three years of engagement with Ugandan LGBTI organizers working transnationally. Therefore, I positioned myself to interrogate the structure and make-up of transnational advocacy, wondering if

Black (Diasporic) queer erasure is a symptom of organizational structure, or indicative of larger, invisibilizing processes. I see that it is both.

Take, for example, a very similar moment in a very different context. I meet Hassan and his friends in Kabalagala one night to watch a football game. Ghana is playing Egypt to qualify for the next World Cup, and (clearly) we're supporting the Black Stars. I'm not feeling all that well, because the 7-hour time difference between NYC and Kampala is still wearing down my body after a week, and not even my favourite beer—Castle Milk Stout—can make me excited to have to walk the 5 km back home after an evening out. During half time, they share a taboo round of beers—given that they are Muslim and usually abstain.

Hassan's friend Mohammad, whose obnoxious personality particularly contrasts the rest of the quiet, respectful group, asks me if I will "bring another Jamaican woman" for him next time I come: one that looks like me, "red-skinned" and "loose haired" and foreign in this part of the continent. He jokes that Jamaican women are the best—licentious like whites but with better rhythm and more respect.

Hassan eyes him suspiciously, aware of the dualism of this insult-compliment style of his flirtation. He also eyes me suspiciously, because at this point we have only known each other for two weeks and this is the first time that I'm hanging out with his friends. I know he wants to know how I'll handle it, but I'm also exhausted and annoyed and my fuse is too short for tipsy men and idiotic comments.

Hassan also knows that I am here to work with underground "feminist" organizations, and already suspects that "feminist" means "homosexual." He makes a quick quip: "She won't be able to bring you any Jamaican women—at least none that are into you. All of her friends are lesbians."

Mohammad, surprised at the suggestion but not surprised at Hassan's provocative character, laughs heartily and says, "Hassan, please, we all know that Jamaican women don't do that shit! They are black like us."[2]

I left not too long after this exchange. The omnipresence of this black+queer erasure damages individuals, communities, and any movement toward a decolonial sexual politic. It is something that I experience consistently, and that is only remedied by deep, honest conversation rooted in connection. These two moments are incredibly different: one occurred with a gay man (Ben) and one with a straight man (Mohammad). One moment was in New York City, with someone who had extensive experience traveling in various Western nations and advocating for queer African visibility. The other moment was in Kampala, with someone who had very little consideration of sexual and gender diversity outside of cisheteropatriarchy. The moments' connections, however, are striking: Black queer experience was invisible to both people. Neither imagine or acknowledge the lived realities of queer, African people of the Diaspora, whether in Jamaica or in the United

States. How is this possible in an era of increasingly interconnected social technologies; unprecedented transnational queer power and visibility?

This erasure exists because, while transnational advocates tokenize select kuchus and use the hypervisibility of their campaigns to reconstitute their own organizational power, the majority of black (and therefore black and queer) bodies are relegated to *death worlds.* Death worlds are spheres of social existence conferred upon certain populations that render them subject to perpetual injury, loss, and death (Mbembé 2003). They are the political formations created for certain bodies to experience the slow death necessary to sustain the life and vitality of bodies of power. Death is physical and seen in homicide victimization[3] and lessened life expectancy.[4] It is a political death: intimidation and assassination has caused the death of Black socialism throughout Africa and its Diaspora. And it is a "social death" (Mbembé, 2003, p. 21), as the fight to physically stay alive negates one's ability to participate politically or hold political status. Simultaneously, those racialized as white are able to access nationalist and supranationalist power and reproduce such divides between empowered (or sovereign) and injured (or subjugated).

The *necropolitics* of homonationalism, therefore, lead to the institutionalization of the erasure of black queer existence. Although a numerically significant minority in the United States, the lives and oppression of those of African descent remain invisible to the world, regardless of queerness but especially heightened when factoring in sexual or gender difference. As state and institutional power "refers and appeals to exception, emergency, and a fictionalized notion of the enemy" (p.16) it labors to produce exactly that: the kuchu exception; the urgency of activism; and the omnipresent African homophobe. This propagation reaffirms the exclusive right of the state (and supranational power) to harm queer, black bodies through carceral politics, militarization and war-mongering, and enforcing perpetual debt. It is through these means that such organizations can ignore the predominant forms of violence experienced by Black, queer people—violence enacted by the state—while materially and rhetorically supporting statist solutions to violence. The ignorance, in turn, allows for organizations and individuals to propagate an image of the United States as progressive, stable, and *safe* for queers. While progress enhances the quality and longevity of life for the homonational, those racialized as Black are relegated to hastened deaths.

We are not inherently invisible or small; black queer subjectivity is invisibilized (verb) and diminished to the status of "unlikely ally" for those who would like a niche.

The death world therefore becomes the only legitimate space for the black body. As black queer existence is erased so too is our resistance. Before introducing his Africanist ideology and connection, David asked, "what would really happen if our prophetic voices, if our truth was ever allowed to be put on center stage?" (originally quoted in Chapter 3). I dedicate this chapter to that line of questioning and ask *what would it look like to center African Diasporic politics, perspectives when strategizing for queer justice?* In order to answer that question, I put forward three organizational models as a projection of what Afro-Diasporic organizing could look like, and how it could positively transform the goals of a transnational queer movement.

Earlier chapters have highlighted the chasm within the transnational human rights regime, that has allowed Ben and others to overlook the experiences most directly related to those in Kampala. In positioning themselves as "brokers" (Thoreson 2014a) that exclusively work on behalf of the "Global South," mainstream transnational organizations uplift and broadcast the virtues of white, Western work in relation to the Black and Brown nations that "require" work. As organizations, they wholly ignore the occurrences of hyperpolicing and surveillance, trauma and death experienced by Black and Brown people *within* the white nation. Simultaneously, they ignore the virtue of the work—largely taken on by people of color—to end such domestic, state violence. This focus perpetuates the idea that 'gay is white and black is homophobic'; phrasing in which 'white' may easily be substituted for 'Western' and 'black,' 'African.' This idea that black people are especially or uniquely homophobic or anti-gay exists as mainstream gay rights movements refuse to acknowledge black queer subjectivities, and decidedly pursue homonationalist campaigns that largely do not affect Black queer people in substantial, positive ways.

This racist construction erases black queer subjectivities and existence as well as the very current presence of homophobia in white cultures. This has been explored to an extent through a look at the *Lawrence v Texas*, 2001 federal overturn of sodomy legislation in the United States (Puar 2007). The history of black anti-homophobia is made evident by a very clear, literal erasure in our memories of the case's fuller name: *Lawrence and Garner v Texas*. Tyron Garner was the black male lover of John Lawrence, the white man whose surname is immortalized as an usher of progress against homophobia. It is Lawrence who earned the right to privacy for consenting adults; it is Garner who is forgotten. The opportunity to remember that in the US—a case involving a black gay man was responsible for overturning historic sodomy legislation was missed.

As Garner is forgotten, so is the long and rich legacy of black contributions to queer liberation. Memorialized (and reproduced) is the way in which progressive people of European descent advocated on our behalf. I will outline, here, three organizational models and extrapolate a transnationalized iteration of the work. In doing so, I highlight three radically transformed conceptualizations of justice, all founded on African principles.

LIBERATORY JUSTICE: MINIMIZING THE ROLES OF RETRIBUTION AND LITIGATION

The Audre Lorde Project is a 24-year-old organization in New York City that works through community organizing. The organization boasts being by and for lesbian, gay, bisexual, two-spirit, transgender, and gender non-conforming (LGBTSTGNC) people of color. The organization features several working groups: TransJustice, which is made up of and for binary and nonbinary transgender people; Third Space, which focuses on wellness resources and handles language and physical accessibility; and Safe OUTside the System, a queer anti-violence collective that responds to hate and police violence in Brooklyn. The organization stresses liberation from harmful institutions and strives to recognize the notion of harm in comprehensive and holistic ways. I choose to introduce this organization here as it is one that I have worked with and gained extensive insight into since 2012.

Campaigning for Safe Neighborhoods

Safe OUTside the System (SOS), operating in Brooklyn, organizes against anti-black and anti-queer hate violence without relying on the police and criminal justice system. One relevant campaign created by SOS is the Safe Neighborhood Campaign (SNC). The SNC focuses on building grassroots understanding and commitment to fostering localized queer safety. For the SNC, SOS members connect with business owners who are interested in expanding their clientele. Members then offer training to the business owner and employees on how to recognize and deescalate violence without calling the police. In the introduction to the training, members pay special attention to the ways in which certain forms of structural violence—racism, nativism, homophobia, and transphobia—are connected. This introduction appeals to business owners, who experience at least one axis of the structural violence and often have little experience making such connections explicit. For Ugandan business owners, examples could be classism/economic deprivation, sexism, or state corruption. Members then share strategies with business owners on avoiding police attention, shielding those victimized or vulnerable, and intervening as bystanders committed to anti-violence.

The SNC is not only possible in Kampala, a less-organized version of it has been attempted. As Olive Minor elaborates from her time with the kuchu community in 2012, a participant she renames *Jackson* began to form relationships with business owners in 2012 in order to create spaces that were safe for kuchus to enjoy nightlife (Minor 2014, p. 12 –27).

> Jackson explained his strategy: he targeted bars around the city and convinced them to invest in a karaoke machine, while hiring him as the host. In exchange,

> he promised to draw in new clientele on evenings when business was slow. Where Jackson began to emcee, kuchus soon followed, and the bars began to make money. (p. 125)

Suffering the loss of a kuchu-owned and managed space, and experiencing significant fragmentation due to the political moment, Jackson engaged in creating safe spaces as his grassroots activism. When bar managers expressed disapproval, Jackson moved the community to another bar. The loss of business resulted in several bar managers changing their disposition, asking Jackson to "tell [his] friends we have no problem with them" (p. 126). While we prefer that the change of heart would not occur solely due to money, we acknowledge that the SNC, as it runs through businesses, opens doors through the incentive of increased patronage. Transnationalizing this campaign would allow for conversations between activists like Jackson and those within SOS to strategize around facilitating the transition from patronage to ideological partnership, sustaining these connections, and promoting safe spaces beyond word-of-mouth.

Community Security

The second relevant piece of work by SOS is not a campaign, but a regular practice of providing community security. Community security is a crucial practice for activists during private events, marches, rallies, and other public forms of protest. However, there are only a limited number of works within social movement studies that mention the practice (Gillham and Noakes 2007; Hui 2015), and even less that center the analysis on it (Hui 2015). No social movement studies scholarship attempts to analyze the practice's potential for transnational diffusion.

Community security involves several roles that all contribute to the safety of protestors: marshals, captains (mobile captains if a march), police negotiators, and a lead security person. The SOS model has been adopted for differing levels of technological access, where walkie-talkies are preferred, but it is also doable without technology. The main job of the community security team is to provide a buffer between protestors and police and/or counter-protestors. Those who sign up for community security are trained in verbal de-escalation, identifying safety, nonverbal communication (body language), and protocol to defer to the hierarchical structure. Unlike most of SOS organizing, which is horizontalist, security sticks to a vertical hierarchy in order to protect those who are within the security team and to make sure that those who are being protected (or shepherded) by the team are best covered.

The first time that I proposed community security training was to Jessie, who I met in June 2014, when the Anti-Homosexuality Act was in effect. As mentioned in Chapter 4, Jessie is an activist who organizes with a group of

LBT people for the advancement and diversification of our understanding of sexual rights. I told Jessie about the origins of and continued need for queer security at events in New York City. In response, Jessie told me about the heightened scrutiny and threat of violence that queer congregations have suffered since 2009 (corroborated by reports from various organizations[5] and governments).[6] Jessie believed that community security was the best way to shield the community from the increased police violence that they faced.

The Audre Lorde Project's goal to "Feel AAIT" (pronounced similarly to *aight*, the Black Vernacular English term, shortening "alright") centers the four movement principles that guide their community organizing: **A**bolitionist, **A**ncestral, **I**nterdependent, and **T**ransformative. These principles, although not articulated as such, are wholly connected to African principles. To embrace *obuntubulamu* (humaneness) is, as *Ubuntu*, to acknowledge that one is only a human being through other human beings. Our actions and treatment of others are to be informed by our interconnectedness. It rejects materialism and individualism: the core arguments against homosexuality made by the anti-gay nationalist. Those of us involved in community organizing centers like ALP, who are and will always be both racialized and queer, embrace the same critiques of mainstream movements that John and Isaac leveraged. The community will reject those that they feel reject, harm, or intentionally avoid helping the community. Rather than framing African people as homophobic, perhaps we could be reframed as often individuophobic: to embrace individualism is to release the communal, the core of how we understand our existence. Our maxim is not I think therefore I am (individualistic) it is *"I am human because I belong"* (Murithi 2006) or *"I am because other people are"* (Tutu 1999).

The organization prioritizes abolition, because the current systems of surveillance and incarceration were created to support colonialism and the continued enslavement of Africans. Abolitionist tactics are inherently crucial for queer communities, as these forms of surveillance, policing, and imprisoning remain central to our experiences throughout the world. In the United States, studies estimate that 47 percent[7] to 61 percent of Black transwomen have been incarcerated. Transpeople, irrespective of race, are more likely to experience incarceration if they identify with the gender binary (FTM, MTF) than if they identify as non-binary (Reisner, Bailey, and Sevelius 2014). Of the five transpeople I interviewed in Kampala for this project (four binary and one nonbinary), four had shared experiences of detention, arrest, and incarceration on at least one occasion. Many kuchus understood police as a site of rampant corruption and extrajudicial (sexual and non-sexual) violence. ALP's position on abolition reorients the queer mission from targeting all efforts on specific criminal legislation, whether introducing new crimes (such as hate crimes) or eradicating old crimes (such as crossdressing, or *impersonation*).[8] Instead, the organization puts forward that there must exist a strong and simultaneous effort to eradicate *the idea of the criminal* from our societies; to break down the false divide of the "degenerate" and the "good citizen."

Interdependence rejects independence as a goal: we do not want a type of sovereignty that foregoes alliance, we want cooperative autonomy. At the end of an event or protest it is not uncommon to hear "we must love one another and protect one another, we have nothing to lose but our chains": the end of a declaration made by Assata Shakur. Even the idea of an action being ancestral is actually communal: our ancestors are not individualized imaginings of with whom *one* actually shares DNA, as commonly used by Europeans. To call Audre Lorde or Harriet Tubman *our* ancestor is not to boast that there is a direct bloodline, it is to say that our histories and paths of resistance are shared: my story is yours, and it is one of love and liberation.

Transformative perspectives were woven into indigenous structures of peacebuilding and solidarity and have also been carried by displaced ancestors when community members cause harm (Morris 2006, Murithi 2006). Transformative justice, as used within the organization, is a vision and practice of justice that puts those most affected by violence at the forefront of eradicating violence. A transformative justice approach rejects prisons and retributive sentencing, as punishment circumvents solutions and reproduces cycles of violence that disproportionately affect vulnerable (impoverished, working class, socially rejected, and racialized) peoples. This approach highlights the universal human capacity to commit acts of harm, while simultaneously acknowledging the socially constructed conditions that entrap people into enacting certain transgressions (like robbery). Therefore, it embraces a politic that rejects the idea that certain peoples are disposable. On the other hand, carceral responses to harm are grounded in such disposability politics: whole groups of people are separated from society and marked as nonessential or as *dangerous classes* (as the 19th century Italian theorist Lombroso famously labeled those outside of the white middle and upper classes). Therefore, transformative strategies embrace comprehensive, non-reactionary analyses in service of creating long-term solutions to societal problems.

Many kuchu Ugandans have undoubtedly mastered personal safety strategies, as they know their home. Transnationalizing community security, SNC, or the principles of abolitionist organizing could potentially collectivize this mastery and allow for events and rallies to include more intentional safety-making, or could pull allies into the movement that are willing to create safe spaces for kuchus as they navigate movement-building in Kampala. Additionally, sharing community-based principles and tactics means integrating more into the wider society, disrupting the narrative that homosexuality is self-serving, new, or un-African (and therefore not a way of our ancestors).

HEALING JUSTICE: ANCESTRAL COMMEMORATION AND FREEDOM FROM OPPRESSIVE INSTITUTIONS

Harriet's Apothecary is a newer organization that also upholds ancestral practices and presents new possibilities of Diaspora-centered organizing. Stemming from the intention to provide services, skill-shares, and self-sustainable medicinal practices—Harriet's Apothecary provides a great example of transnational connection that is rooted both in identity politics and interdependence. Founded by Nigerian healer Adaku Utah, the organization began as a small, pop-up art venture in 2014, blending the liberationist vision of Harriet Tubman with an apothecary—a center where community members can find natural medicine and holistic health consultations. Utah states that, "like our courageous ancestor [Harriet Tubman], we intend to expand access to health and healing resources that support our community, specifically Black, Indigenous and PoC folks, in their journeys toward freedom." In that intention, the Apothecary began to expand opportunities to an intergenerational and multi-modal cast of healers.

Harriet's Apothecary has since mushroomed, spreading from a three healer-led grouping in one city to a mobile village of over twenty Black cis- and trans- identified healers in December 2015. Their website artfully states:

> Harriet's Apothecary healers are children from the lands of Nigeria, Haiti, Gullah, Trinidad, Jamaica, South Carolina, Louisiana and Brooklyn. . . . We want our healing village to be a space where we can feel into the pain that has been cast into our lives, and summon up creative opportunities to authentically invoke healing. We want to support our community in making plant-based, Earth-based, medicine potent enough to seep deep to unveil our sources of power and span wide enough to hold and heal the spaces that beg to be heard.

These healers provide wellness and therapeutic services to queer people of color throughout the United States, including in Ferguson, Missouri, in 2014 and began their transnationalizing effort in Komye, Haiti, in April 2015. By March of 2016, representatives of the Apothecary spoke at the United Nations and by June, they joined *Astraea's CommLabs,* a convening of LGBTI activists for skillshares and conversations about the role of communications technology in movement building in Durban, South Africa. Astraea Center for Lesbian Justice supported the Durban trip and has similarly supported lesbian organizing in Kampala, funding FAR-UG in 2014. Sustained support of transnational queer, healing work, however, is thus far unprecedented.

Importantly, only participants of African descent ever brought up *healing* as a priority. For example, while homonationalist conceptualizations limit progress to law-changing and inclusion into citizenship, David believed that his work is "about this kind of healing of the continent and the Diaspora." Oliver, one of the longest standing and most prominent kuchu activists in

Kampala, shared with me countless stories of activist exhaustion and illness. The movement cannot sustain if the sustenance of those building it is not supported, yet, health, healing, and strength-building were never raised as a priority by transnational LGBT rights organizations. Healing rhetoric appears as a radical departure from mainstream, cross-world work. However, if it is indeed radical, that is fine: radical implies that it is at the root of an issue. *The point is that it is possible* to transnationalize and prioritize support of queer wellness.

Access to health care has been a perplexing struggle for kuchu Ugandans. Although there are kuchu and allied health-care workers in various fields, the Anti-Homosexuality Bill complicated service provision. Many interpreted that the section pertaining to "aiding and abetting homosexuality," as originally proposed in 2009, criminalized the action of providing care to kuchus without reporting them to the police. Therefore, Oliver said that this severely limited those who were known to be allies, as economic standing is so precarious that no one could afford critical inspection in their workplace. The second blow came when the World Bank, the United States, Sweden, Norway, Denmark, and the Netherlands collectively withheld over $100m USD in aid or loans, a withholding that disproportionately affected the health-care sector of Uganda. Overlooked in the West's course of "punishing" Uganda for its treatment of LGBTI people was the fact that LGBTI people *are* Ugandans, who also lost their jobs due to the sanctions and faced increased hostility as peers held their queerness (hyperindividualism and special rights) responsible for the loss of aid for the nation. Isaac remarked on this moment as a "double ended sword"; as their nation suffers due to aid cuts, so too do their businesses. He projected an increase in taxation of his internet café *and* more scapegoating of the community.

The Audre Lorde Project also commits to providing access to wellness spaces, both with traditional healing and Western practices. ALP features a program called "Third Space," specifically devoted to facilitating health and wellness access for queer people of color, who, despite living in one of the wealthiest nations in the world, largely cannot visit a hospital or choose an ambulance without risking further financial instability. Urban poverty, as experienced by so many black queer people in central Brooklyn, exposes the population to slow death—the physical wearing out of the population through capitalist, structural subordination and governmentality (Berlant 2007). This is the intersection of economic and state violence that occurs nationally and globally for people of African descent, regardless of nationality.

Urban poverty is also the condition through which queer/kuchu organizers in Uganda are working. As Black queer organizations in New York begin to prioritize free access to wellness spaces—we expand our understanding of our being past visions/responses to the inevitability of early death and into the possibility of vitality. We make room to look beyond HIV prevention and into well-being—connecting networks of acupuncture and reiki practitioners, massage therapists, yogis, and capoeiristas—people of color who ground their work in the desire to uplift those of the African Diaspora. The Audre Lorde Project, in particular, prioritizes integrating these spaces into every large scale event, from the annual "Bed-Stuy Pride" to the Community Freestyle I mentioned earlier. Ancestral teachings have shown us that the only way to survive poverty (amongst other conditions) is through interdependence. Holding on to that legacy, the organization has thrived.

A model of transnational cooperation that extends beyond homonationalism—spreading marriage and changing laws—would recognize this potential and seek ways to make it work. Kampala, a metropolitan area of nearly two million people, undoubtedly has queer and queer friendly people in all fields of health and wellness. However, necropolitical governmentality and poverty hold most kuchus from accessing these spaces. Transnational cooperation could inspire creative methods of connecting kuchus to needed resources, but in its current, cross-world formation, these connections are undersupported or altogether missed.

CONCLUSION

I'll conclude with an experience that seized connection. I originally "met" Oliver via that social media platform Twitter. As is common with a few, well-traveled queer Ugandans and more active queer organizers in New York City, he and I shared several followers, and had a few mutual, "in real life" comrades. I messaged him about a month before I would head back out to Uganda in 2014, and he told me that he would actually be in NYC for a week beforehand. As SOS was working on an annual event called the Community Freestyle, I thought it was actually a perfect chance for him to attend an event where LGBTQ people of color talk/strategize about police violence and staying safe in a rapidly gentrifying central Brooklyn.

In this convening, we shared an analysis of how economic and spatial violence—the forced displacement of people of color through economic means—affects queer Black and Latino people in the neighborhoods within central Brooklyn. This largely looks like white (LGBT and straight) people moving in and inviting more police presence in order to protect them or their businesses. It looks like "Broken Windows"-guided law enforcement: hyper-policing minor infractions, and using such infractions to escalate and quicken the removal of Black and brown bodies from the hood. It also looks like us, very simply, not being able to afford rent and being pushed farther east in Brooklyn or outside of the borough entirely.

In a remarkably different mode of interaction than what I had shared with Ben, Oliver was excited to join, help out, and learn about queer Black issues in the urban US. We became friends and went on to later spend time in Kampala. The basis of our connection is a shared commitment to uplift our people: people of African descent. Being such, we've given each other numerous opportunities to connect with organizers doing this work—whether in NYC or in Kampala—and to expand the understandings of what "queer issues" are for anyone in our wake.

It is through this framework that I argue that Diaspora-centered connections can form organizational strategies that are relevant to an East African context. Collectives such as the Audre Lorde Project and Harriet's Apothecary have created not just relevant analyses, but also *strategies of protest and organizing* from the intersections. These intersectional strategies would "build the capacity" of any organization in the Diaspora to accomplish their goals in a way that a relationship based on funding simply cannot. For example, if an organization wishes to better the life chances of their local community, sharing campaigns that center *wellness* is a culturally relevant step.

Unlike Diaspora-centered organizing, cross-world advocacy reproduces hegemonic, nationalist power, and therefore limits the reach that gender and sexual justice organizers should have. Homonationalism in transnational advocacy transmits the message that justice begins when anti-sodomy legislation is overturned and governments stop rejecting LGBTI people and start acknowledging and integrating them. It also, counterproductively in African contexts, reifies the image that the best allies for LGBTI people are white people (queer or straight). The enemy, or inherently anti-gay, is the Black neighbor, citizen, and government. In this way, homonationalism ignores anti-black *systems* of violence and completely misses the intersections that create culturally relevant movement strategies. It leads to the symbolic, material, and physical abandonment of Black spaces.

Black queer erasure in transnational organizing and imagining occurs while we suffer both urgent and longstanding needs. While countries like the United States and South Africa are held as progressive nations for "LGBT rights," one transwoman is murdered every month in South Africa[9] and roughly two each month in the United States.[10] Despite 'progressive' legislation, at least eleven black transpeople were killed in the first seven months of 2018 (Ring 2018). Of the sixteen known murders of transpeople in the United States in 2018, two of the victims were white (despite the racial category representing over 60 percent of the nation). These racialized experiences are never shared by those who boast this idea of "progress," even though the recipients of such narratives would also be racialized as Black within the United States. When progress is marked solely by legal change, there follows a diminished importance of "foundational categories that are less abstract and more tactile, such as life and death" (Mbembé 2003, p. 14). That is to say, physical markers of human and social progress, such as life expectancy, are cast aside in favor of neoliberal, rights-based conceptualizations.

Accepting this regime of understanding results in undervaluing the potential fruitfulness of Black Diasporic connections. Therefore, this chapter attempts several connections: one of blackness with queerness; one of continental Africa with its Diaspora; and one of queer politics with anti-imperialist politics. Despite the relatively static methods of mainstream transnational organizing, alternative organizational models can be transnationalized to better support kuchu movement building. An Afro-Diasporic centered organizing structure would grow from the concatenations building between the death worlds of and within New York City and Kampala.

NOTES

1. Field Notes, New York City, November 2012.
2. Field Notes, Kampala, Uganda, June 30, 2013.
3. The National Coalition of Anti-Violence Programs reported in 2013 that nearly 90 percent of all LGBTQ homicide victims were people of color.
4. An intersectional view of life expectancy reveals that those living at the margins of marginalized identities, such as Black transwomen, are estimated to have less than half of the life expectancy of majority groups. Although it is impossible to have a perfect figure, due to the lack of collecting gender-identity census data, the current estimated life expectancy is 35 years.
5. For detailed information regarding police brutality and vigilante violence, read the SMUG 2016 Report titled "And That's How I Survived Being Killed."
6. U.S. Department of State Report, 2016.
7. National Gay and Lesbian Task Force, 2011 Report, "Injustice at Every Turn: A Report of the National Transgender Discrimination Survey."
8. Olive Melissa Minor (2014) found that two of her participants, Tyra and Wendell, had been arrested for "impersonating the opposite sex" (p. 239).
9. Astraea Lesbian Foundation for Justice Report on South Africa LGBTI, 2016.
10. There were 27 known murders of transwomen in 2016 and in 2017, 20 of the victims were black. Three were white (or white passing).

Conclusion

The Anti-Homosexuality Bill of 2009 propelled Uganda to the forefront of global media. In its initial manifestation, the Bill threatened to penalize "aggravated homosexuality" with the death penalty. The media attention earned by the proposed legislation opened avenues for transnational cooperation and communication between US-based Human and LGBTI Rights organizations and Ugandan kuchus. My research has focused on this transnational relationship as it interacts with the dynamic of organizing in the midst of a national project of sexual repression.

Transnational advocacy, which aims to empower LGBTI rights activism, actually restructures and, in some cases, limits local movements. This problematic dynamic exists in partnerships between Uganda and organizations based in the United States. I found that these limitations begin with a philosophical and structural disjuncture between American and Ugandan groups, but also largely result from power differentials that remain unaddressed and therefore recapitulated. The bureaucracy of such transnational organizations divests from alternative forms of organizing, and instead reinvests in small networks of power that center around the most powerful institutions and governments in the world. While transnational efforts may be made to support creative, religious, or cultural work, such efforts are instead focused on litigation, reporting, and high-leveled conversations.

Kuchus assert their ideas on actions that may be efficacious within Uganda, yet are asked to speak in "the language of human rights" in order to receive attention and support from the regime. This language, in turn, deradicalized the social movement and constructed a narrow set of goals that led to hyper-factionalization and increased vulnerability, due to the nationalized visibility. Transnational partners marginalize the African perspectives, in favor of requiring that those who seek partnership instead learn *the trans-*

national language (that most legible to the preexisting structure). This marginalization occurs as Ugandans are imagined as "lucky" to land temporary employment with transnational organizations and are relegated to "regional" or "local" representatives, rather than those with internationally relevant expertise. The differentiation between those with experience (kuchus) and those with expertise (white, transnational worker in the US) is a stark reminder that national and racial privilege remain the elements of foremost importance to the regime. Despite rhetorical attempts of the transnational human rights worker to heed advice of those "on the ground," the lack of questioning *and action* around *who* gets access to this type of work and who ultimately has the power to make decisions hurts the kuchu organizers who have been engaged for some time, who quite desperately desire solidarity amongst autonomous bodies, rather than patronization.

On the other hand, the patronization of the movement has created infighting between activist factions. Factionalization, as explained in Chapter 4 is one such manifestation of these divisions and began in the mid-2000s, when SMUG, FARUG, and other long-standing organizations began to receive funding. The factionalization expanded in the wake of the Anti-Homosexuality Bill, when unprecedented financial support and attention poured into Uganda. With this transnational attention also came the phenomenon of briefcase organizations, where groupings of people learned the language of human rights and treated it as a job in and of itself, regardless of their own sexuality or if they were indeed interested in doing activist work. In order to ensure that funding was not shared with such briefcase organizations, transnational funders and brokers increasingly relied on established networks: a reliance that further concentrated resources and legitimation to a small minority of already-supported, largely middle-class kuchus.

The newest, least supported organizations remained unintelligible to the regime, yet desiring of US funding. Jessie described to me, when we met, his surprise that we were indeed meeting. When I asked why, he said because usually resources were not shared and I, along with journalists, funders, and any outside attention, were imagined as potential resources. This, I found interesting, as it satisfied my curiosity regarding how and why it took *so long* and genuine persistence to connect with organizations that were outside of the most well-known core of kuchu activists.

The financial support that largely middle-class kuchus were suspected to receive did not trickle down, leading to betrayal. The most insidious betrayals, such as blackmail or selling information to the government and newspapers were described to me by Oliver and other prominent activists. Reports of this phenomenon is corroborated by other research in the area (Kiragu and Nyong'o 2005; Minor 2014). Although not commonly attended to in queer African studies, "the fact that LGBTI people cut across the socio-economic divide places great challenge and opportunity for blackmail" (Kiragu and

Nyong'o 2005), creating a climate permeated by suspicion (Minor 2014), caginess, and fear. Most remarkably, such class tensions result in a hesitation to extend support and opportunity to newcomers, the very action for which the core and umbrella organizations are sponsored.

Altogether, these issues are indicative of the development of a new, competitive economy for kuchu activism. However new this may be when applied to queer organizing, this is, as Minor notes, "a well-worn economic strategy—particularly for educated, middle-class Ugandans whose avenues to well-paid, stable employment in other sectors have been blocked by nepotism, exploitation, and an oversaturated labor market with few other opportunities" (p.167). Museveni's drive to stay in power for over thirty years provided opportunities for this neoliberal economy to develop in Uganda. As the government accepted Structural Adjustment Programs, rapid privatization and NGOization swept Uganda, leaving the responsibilities of most social, military, and health developments outside of the government's power or purview. After this political economic shift, a thousand NGOs quickly took hold of Uganda in the mid-1990s (Lyons 1998, p. 194; Minor 2014). This number has skyrocketed, which even ordinary Ugandans (outside of economics or political fields) have witnessed firsthand: as of 2018, *there are 13,000 registered NGOs.* This rapid proliferation creates a tension between the government as it represents the spheres of Ugandan life that the government has little control over. In "The NGO-ization of Resistance" Roy states:

> Most large-funded NGOs are financed and patronized by aid and development agencies, which are, in turn, funded by Western governments, the World Bank, the UN and some multinational corporations. Though they may not be the very same agencies, they are certainly part of the same loose, political formation that oversees the neoliberal project and demands the slash in government spending in the first place.

Therefore, we can witness these legislative assertions, over who can access citizenship and who must be sacrificed in order to build an allegiant citizenry, as the government's attempt at sovereignty. Brilliantly, Mbembé defines the decisions around who "to kill or to allow to live" as the "fundamental attributes" of sovereignty (Mbembé 2003, p. 1 –2). Such attempts are thus logically (yet inexcusably) over-asserted in this moment when foreign aid contributed to 80 percent of "development" initiatives (Branch 2011, p. 84) and around 50 percent of the country's budget in 2009 (Babyenda 2014; IED 2015). This economy not only recreates spirals of debt, but also anxieties that manifest as a toxic and virulent animus against deviating sexuality.

Altogether, the takeaway of this book is absolutely not that transnational organizing is inherently useless or hurtful; it is that a transnational solidarity movement needs to be cognizant of power and based in shared consciousness, not in patronage. The mainstream movement, in its current formation, attends rhetorically to issues of privilege, but is limited as an institution. This is why participants, such as Matt, state that they "have certain services to offer, particularly like trainings around writing a shadow report, or giving access to the United Nations, but like we're not going to force you to do that, *you have to want to work with us.*" This reveals that despite conversations about partnership and shared efforts, there is a structure that the regime rests on, that "local" activists can choose to access or not. Despite the effort that mainstream human rights organizations make to highlight that they need to receive "advice," ultimately the structure is not amenable to different needs around the world, it is only enabled to work in a narrow manner that stresses mutuality, rather than redistribution. As Lisa Duggan notes, this is endemic within neoliberalism, in which the "overall impact has been the upward redistribution of resources and the reproduction of stark patterns of social inequality" (2003, p. xiv). Thoreson (2014) from a more microstructural viewpoint, describes that this crystallization ultimately occurred at IGLHRC, which retained an institutional character despite the changing body of activists who worked with the organization. When an organization forms, the overall politic remains intact, even while the politics of the individual brokers may differ. A similar phenomenon occurs for local organizations as they attempt to fit into a hyperstructured transnational sphere.

Therefore, as local organizations vie for international attention and funding, they restructure their movement goals and strategies in order to best attract desired partners. John summarized his frustrations with the current climate, stating: "In 2004, we were empowered. In 2014, we are *financed.*" He described a 2004 that was not marked by such anti-gay anger: In his account, "[hatred] was not ignited, people knew gays existed, but they did not care." He attributes the detonation to "commandos" who are "so aggressive how they want money." Therefore, he shifted the blame from the structural issues to the missteps of individual kuchus, who compromised the safety of the LGBTI community in order to seek transnational visibility and funding. He reflected fondly on the times when organizing and merrymaking occurred, largely facilitated by an Italian immigrant and pub-owner. However, as I searched for information regarding the name he gave me, *Pietro*, the reporting that I found disrupts this nostalgic account that no one cared. A *New Vision* reporter in August 2002 wrote:

> Ethics and Integrity Minister Miria Matembe yesterday named Mama Mia Restaurant Sax Pub as one of the pubs promoting sexual immorality in Kampala city. Matembe, who was addressing a weekly government press briefing in Kampala, said Mama Mia, an Italian restaurant close to Tourist Hotel, is where homosexuality takes place. . . . "What happens at Sax pub at night is terrible. I don't know where this country is heading. There is too much immorality all around us. Homosexuality, lesbianism, name it," she said.[1]

The anxiety, therefore, is anything but new. Whether or not there existed a different level of populist hostility has not yet been explored, and would require operationalizing hostility (perhaps in number of violent attacks). Importantly, this data would be impossible without the work that groups like SMUG do, as researching and documenting abuses is an aspect of their activism. However, the disjuncture between the mainstream and John's counter-narrative reveals something far more important, that this book took up: the discord between forms of activism (grassroots versus institutionalized) has inspired mistrust and factionalization of a movement that desperately needs cohesion. The narrative of receiving "funding from the West" actually causes local discord both *among* kuchu organizations and *between* kuchu and non-LGBT Ugandans, who imagine the new philosophies associated with the movement as selling out, un-African, or anti-Ugandan. More concretely, the increase in parliamentary discussion, and the fervor with which the next ethics and integrity minister monitored homosexuality, does, in part, support John's assertion.

I refer to this development as "the economies of queer inclusion" because political economic anxieties are ever present in Kampala. These anxieties shape the movement: who can and does participate in movement building, how participation works (and doesn't work), as well as who fights back against kuchus and how it is codified as an anti-imperial effort. We would be amiss to avoid the very real economy that has been created to further gay rights, that introduced itself to Uganda in the mid-2000s. The Anti-Homosexuality Bill was quite clearly drafted as an anxious response to the threat of such an economy moving through Uganda and shifting its culture. Explicit references to the increased access to information technologies and the presence of stronger, foreign currencies appear in the introduction to the Bill and the media reporting after 2009 (Sadgrove et al. 2012).

Despite this transnational economy and the reactive tensions, I do imagine that transnational organizing is possible. The previous chapter outlines just two forms of community organizing that can be transnationalized, as the principles that guide the organizing are Diasporic (and therefore, inherently transnational). Queer initiatives to support wellness, self-determination, and community engagement have ready applications in the Kampala context. While there are already organizing efforts being generated in Kampala, by Ugandans and for Ugandans, there are also possibilities for practical diffusion that kuchu organizers could adopt, if they desired. This way of connecting could occur without a foreign presence that replicates settler or indirect colonial methods, and therefore have greater potential to take hold. However, the ultimate need for kuchus are for them to have their own opportunities for self-sustenance so that they may engage in community building, which cannot occur without a transnational politics that puts redistribution and reparation at the forefront; that favors reparation and debt forgiveness to continued patronage and the savior-complex that has arisen with the current, neoliberal human rights paradigm.

SCHOLARLY CONTRIBUTIONS

The book contributes an understanding of transnationalism *vis a vis* the construction of LGBTI communities, racial othering, and nationalist countermovements. It identifies the (i)NGOization of LGBTI justice movements—not the mere presence of diverse sexualities and genders—as the impetus of the nationalist crackdown in Uganda. The text also describes the ways in which these transnational relationships form within both formal, UN-centered transnational structures and the transnational "grassroots" (actors who consider themselves independent of these formal structures).

Social movement scholars will also appreciate the contributions to our understanding of visibility strategies and coalition-building. Prior scholarship on African LGBTI movements has addressed the strategic dilemmas of South African LGBTI social movement organizations (Currier 2012); the historical forms of homosexualities in Africa (Hoad 2007); and the heterosexualization of the continent (Epprecht 2008). None, however, have offered an extensive analysis on how transnational alliances affect these local assemblages. Currier's research for *Out in Africa*, the closest scholarly text, concludes with a call for a theoretical and methodological consideration of transnationalism. Importantly, she also notes that southern Africa is the region with thus far the most comprehensive literary presence in African LGBT studies. This book on Uganda, an East African nation, is timely and distinctive.

Research for this text began in 2011, which makes it a seven-year analytical journey, to date of this writing. When I began this research, there were no academic texts yet published dedicated to this movement. There were relatively few works of investigative or engaged journalism, Kapya Kaoma (2009) really stood out, in that sense. However, there has since grown a body of works that analyze different phenomena in the same moment and movement: when religion fosters hate and becomes law (Kaoma 2009); when new ideological mobilizations become understood as tradition (Cheney 2012, Nyanzi 2013; Tamale 2008); when good intentions become "homocapitalism" (Rao 2015). However, it is my position that an analysis of an issue of this scope requires *time*. Thus far, very few scholars have given their time to investigating, developing, and analyzing this case, although brilliant scholarship has explored sexuality in Uganda more generally (see references to Sylvia Tamale). Until this year, all works dedicated to queer Uganda, from any angle, have been short features: a blog post, an article, a chapter within a book. There has only been one other book-length text on the subject, and it is an unpublished dissertation (Minor 2014). Minor witnessed incredibly similar phenomena throughout her ethnography, which had a term of fieldwork that ended just as mine began. Unfortunately, it was not until 2018 that I was made aware and received access to the text. However, in incorporating her data extensively, it is my hope that the two works viewed together can provide insight into movement-making before, during, and after the international human rights regime overwhelms a budding form of organizing.

An Invitation for Future Analyses

A persistent question of mine, that I was not able to pursue during this research, was whether or not queer justice movements in countries with African majorities, once colonized by the British, are better off without the transnational regime? I held the Bahamas in mind, which rid itself of the British colonial law in 1991, without forming a single "LGBTI Rights" NGO; without funding from the Core. What tactics were they able to employ? What strategies were mobilized? Were they less likely to face questioning of the authenticity of their Blackness and queerness? I would cherish such a work that embraced a political economic perspective while reflecting on this (assumed) mobilization.

Additionally, Uganda estimates having between 37 and 44 million residents. Only roughly two million people live in Kampala, yet all of the analyses of queer movement making focus on Kampala. This is a clear limitation of this work, which I would invite the opportunity to remedy. When in Uganda, I connected with activists in Mbarara and Jinja. There are many other areas, with very different geographies and industries that may feature LGBTI movements with diverse formations. Although many of Kampala-based activists describe their gravitation to Kampala as informed by the availability of queer social life, there are undoubtedly queer Ugandans creating community, safety, and self-determination outside of Kampala. An extensive analysis of rural or Northern queer life and organizing would be fantastic, as such forms of organizing have not drawn attention from international funders. The social classes of individual kuchus are much more likely to be held relatively constant. What are the dynamics in such locales?

Altogether, works on sexual justice organizing expand our understanding of the relationship between identity formation, movement-making, and state repression. We can further nuance our understandings of sexual citizenship and state violence by interrogating the queer community-making around the world. In doing so, we face the possibility of creating strengthened, supranational connections (through Diaspora), and ideally bettering our own accountability processes, as national, transnational, or non-national actors.

NOTE

1. *New Vision* Reporter, 2002 "Matembe Names Kampala Homo Pubs."

Bibliography

Alexander, M. J. (1994). Not just (any) body can be a citizen: The politics of law, sexuality and postcoloniality in Trinidad and Tobago and the Bahamas. *Feminist Review*, *48*(1), 5–23.

———. (2006). *Pedagogies of Crossing: Meditations on Feminism, Sexual Politics, Memory, and the Sacred* (Perverse Modernities). Durham: Duke University Press.

Allen, T., & Heald, S. (2004). HIV/AIDS Policy in Africa: What has worked in Uganda and what has failed in Botswana?. *Journal of International Development*, *16*(8), 1141–1154.

Altman, L. K. (1982). New Homosexual Disorder Worries Officials, *The New York Times*.

Anzaldúa, G. E. (2013). Now let us shift ... the path of conocimiento ... inner work, public acts. In *This bridge we call home* (pp. 554–592). New York: Routledge.

Arellano-López, S., & Petras, J. F. (1994). Non-Governmental Organizations and Poverty Alleviation in Bolivia. *Development and Change*, 25(3), 555–568.

Astraea (2016). South Africa LGBTI: Landscape Analysis of Political, Economic & Social Conditions. Astraea Lesbian Foundation for Justice. Accessed 25 July 2018: http://www.astraeafoundation.org/uploads/files/publications/AstraeaUSAID.SouthAfrica.04_11_16.pdf.

Avert. (2011a). The history of AIDS in the United States Retrieved May, 2011, from http://www.avert.org/aids-history-america.htm.

Avert. (2011b). HIV and AIDS in Uganda, from http://www.avert.org/aids-uganda.htm#contentTable0.

Bacchetta P and J Haritaworn. (2011). There are many transatlantics: Homonationalism, homotransnationalism and feminist-queer-trans of color theories and practices. In: Davis K and Evans M (eds) *Transatlantic Conversations: Feminism as Traveling Theory*. Aldershot: Ashgate, 127–143.

Bahati, D. (2009). *Anti-Homosexuality Bill*. Retrieved from http://wthrockmorton.com/wp-content/uploads/2009/10/anti-homosexuality-bill-2009.pdf.

Banerjee, T. (2013). Media, Movements, and Mobilization: Tea Party Protests in the United States, 2009–2010, in Patrick G. Coy (ed.) *Research in Social Movements, Conflicts and Change* (36), Emerald Group Publishing Limited, pp. 39–75.

Battle, J. et al. (2000). Say it Loud, I'm Black and I'm Proud. Black Pride Survey 2000. The Policy Institute of the National Gay and Lesbian Task Force. http://www.thetaskforce.org/static_html/downloads/reports/reports/SayItLoudBlackAndProud.pdf.

Baudh, S. (2008). Human Rights and the Criminalisation of Consensual Same-Sex Sexual Acts In the Commonwealth, South and Southeast Asia *TARSHI*. New Delhi: The South and Southeast Asia Resource Centre on Sexuality.

BBC. (2011). Transcript Philip Hammond Interview. *The Andrew Marr Show*.

Bell, D., & Binnie, J. (2000). *The sexual citizen: Queer politics and beyond*. Cambridge: Polity Press.

———. (2002). Sexual Citizenship. *Handbook of lesbian and gay studies*.

———. (2006). Geographies of sexual citizenship. *Political Geography*.

Bennett, W. L. (2005). "Social Movements Beyond Borders: Organization, Communication, and Political Capacity in Two Eras of Transnational Activism," in Donatella della Porta and Sidney Tarrow eds, *Transnational Protest and Global Activism*. Boulder CO: Rowman & Littlefield, 2005, pp. 203–226.

Berlant, L. (2007). Slow death (sovereignty, obesity, lateral agency). *Critical Inquiry*, *33*(4), 754–780.

Bernstein, M. (1997). "Celebration and Suppression: The Strategic Uses of Identity by the Lesbian and Gay Movement." *American Journal of Sociology* 103(3): 531–65.

Blackstone, W. (1916). *Commentaries on the Laws of England*. Vol. I.

Blee, K. and Ashley Currier. (2005). "Character-Building: The Dynamics of Emerging Social Movement Groups." *Mobilization: An International Journal* 10(1): 101–16.

———. (2011). Ethics beyond the IRB: An introductory essay. *Qualitative Sociology*, *34*(3), 401.

Boli, J. and George Thomas. 1997. "World Culture in the World Polity: A Century of Non-Governmental Organization." *American Sociological Review* 62: 171–190.

Bompani, B. (2016). "'For god and for my country': Pentecostal-Charismatic churches and the framing of a new political discourse in Uganda." In *Public Religion and the Politics of Homosexuality in Africa* (pp. 31–46). New York: Routledge.

Boswell, J. (1980). *Homosexuality: Gay People in Western Europe from the Beginning of the Christian Era to the Fourteenth Century*. Chicago: The University of Chicago Press, 100, 101.

Boyd, A. (2002). *Daily Afflictions: The Agony of Being Connected to Everything in the Universe*. New York: W. W. Norton.

Branch, Adam. 2011. *Displacing Human Rights: War and Intervention in Northern Uganda*. Oxford: Oxford University Press.

Burroway, J. (2014). Ugandan President, MPs At Odds Over Anti-Homosexuality Act. (Accessed through http://www.boxturtlebulletin.com/tag/red-pepper).

Buss, D., & Herman, D. (2003). *Globalizing Family Values. The Christian Rights in International Politics*. Minneapolis: University of Minnesota Press.

Cage, K., & Evans, M. (2003). *Gayle: The language of kinks and queens: A history and dictionary of gay language in South Africa*. Jacana Media.

Canaday, M. (2003). Building a straight state: Sexuality and social citizenship under the 1944 GI Bill. *The Journal of American History*, *90*(3), 935–957.

———. (2009). *The Straight State: Sexuality and Citizenship in Twentieth-Century America.*. Princeton: Princeton University Press.

Cantú, L., Naples, N. A., & Vidal-Ortiz, S. (2009). *The sexuality of migration: Border crossings and Mexican immigrant men*. New York: NYU Press.

Carmin, J. and Deborah B. Balser. (2002). "Selecting Repertoires of Action in Environmental Movement Organizations." *Organization and Environment* 15(4): 365–88.

Chasin, A. (2000). *Selling out: The lesbian and gay movement goes to market*. New York: St. Martin's.

Cheney, K. (2012). "Locating Neocolonialism, 'Tradition,' and Human Rights in Uganda's 'Gay Death Penalty.'" *African Studies Review, 55*(2), 77–95.

Clark, Ann Marie, Elisabeth J. Friedman and Kathryn Hochstetler. (1998). "The Sovereign Limits of Global Civil Society: A Comparison of NGO Participation in UN World Conferences on the Environment, Human Rights, and Women." *World Politics* 51: 1–35.

Cohen, W. (1970). The Colonized as Child: British and French Colonial Rule. *African Historical Studies, 3*(2), 427–431.

Collins, P. H. (2000). "It's All in the Family: Intersections of Gender, Race, and Nation." In *Decentering the Center: Philosophy for a Multicultural, Postcolonial, and Feminist World*, ed. Uma Narayan and Sandra Harding, 156–76. Bloomington: Indiana University Press.

———. (2004). *Black sexual politics: African Americans, gender, and the new racism*. New York: Routledge.

Cossman, B. (2007). *Sexual citizens: The legal and cultural regulation of sex and belonging.* Stanford: Stanford University Press.

Crenshaw, K. (1989). "Demarginalizing the Intersection of Race and Sex: A Black Feminist Critique of Antidiscrimination Doctrine, Feminist Theory, and Antiracist Politics." *University of Chicago Legal Forum* 139–67.

———. (1991). "Mapping the Margins: Intersectionality, Identity Politics, and Violence against Women of Color." *Stanford Law Review* 43(6):1241–79.

Currier, A. (2007). The Visibility of Sexual Minority Movement Organizations in Namibia and South Africa. University of Pittsburgh (dissertation).

———. (2012). *Out in Africa: LGBT Organizing in Namibia and South Africa.* Minneapolis: University of Minnesota Press.

de Beauvoir, S. (1949). Le deuxième sexe, 2 vols. *Paris: Gallimard, 1*, 949. Translated as *The Second Sex* by HM Parshley. Harmondsworth: Penguin. 1953.

Donnelly, J. (1986). *International Human Rights: A Regime Analysis.* International Organization. Cambridge: Cambridge University Press.

Doornbos, M. R. (1976). Ethnicity, Christianity, and the Development of Social Stratification in Colonial Ankole, Uganda. *The International Journal of African Historical Studies, 9*(4), 555–575.

Downey, G. L. (1986). "Ideology and the Clamshell Identity: Organizational Dilemmas in the Anti-Nuclear Power Movement." *Social Problems* 33(5): 357–73.

Duggan, L. (2003). *The Twilight of Equality? Neoliberalism, Cultural Politics and the Attack on Democracy.* Boston: Beacon Press.

Einwohner, R. L. (2006). "Identity Work and Collective Action in a Repressive Context: Jewish Resistance on the 'Aryan Side' of the Warsaw Ghetto." *Social Problems* 53(1): 38–56.

Epprecht, M. (1998). "The 'Unsaying' of Indigenous Homosexualities in Zimbabwe: Mapping a Blindspot in African Masculinity." *Journal of Southern African Studies, 24*(4), 631–651.

———. (2005). Black skin, 'cowboy' masculinity: A genealogy of homophobia in the African nationalist movement in Zimbabwe to 1983. *Culture, health & sexuality.*

———. (2008). *Heterosexual Africa? The History of an Idea from the Age of Exploration to the Age of AIDS.* Athens: Ohio University Press.

Evans, D. (2002). Sexual citizenship: The material construction of sexualities.

Gamson, W. A. (1975). *The Strategy of Social Protest.* Homewood, IL: Dorsey Press.

Gillham, P.F. and Noakes, J. A. (2007). "'More than a March in a Circle': Transgressive protests and the limits of negotiated management." *Mobilization: An International Quarterly* 12(4): 341–357.

Gosine, A. (2009). "Speaking sexuality: The heteronationalism of MSM." In *Sexuality, social exclusion and human rights*, edited by C. Barrow, M. de Bmin, and R. Carr, 95–115. Kingston, Jamaica: Ian Rändle Publishers.

Greenberg, G. (2007). Gay by Choice? The Science of Sexual Identity. Retrieved from http://motherjones.com/politics/2007/08/gay-choice-science-sexual-identity?page=2.

Gupta, A. (2008). *This Alien Legacy: The Origins of "Sodomy" Laws in British Colonialism.* New York: Human Rights Watch.

Herrera, Y. M., & Braumoeller, B. F. (2004). Symposium: Discourse and content analysis. *Qualitative Methods*, 2(1), 15–19.

Hoad, N. (1999). Between the white man's burden and the white man's disease: tracking lesbian and gay human rights in Southern Africa.

———. (2007). *African Intimacies: Race, Homosexuality, and Globalization.* Minneapolis: University of Minnesota Press.

Hollander, M. (2009). Gay Rights in Uganda: Seeking to Overturn Uganda's Anti-Sodomy Laws. *Virginia Journal of International Law, 50*(1), 219–266.

HRW (Human Rights Watch). (2014). Uganda: Anti-Homosexuality Act's Heavy Toll. https://www.hrw.org/news/2014/05/14/uganda-anti-homosexuality-acts-heavy-toll

Hui, V. T. B. (2015). The protests and beyond. *Journal of Democracy*, 26(2), 111–121.

IED (2015). International Evaluation Group. Joint Evaluation of Budget Support to Uganda. Final Report. Volume 2, May 2015. Accessed at: https://ec.europa.eu/europeaid/sites/devco/files/strategic-evaluation-cooperation-ec-bs-uganda-1344-annex1-201505_en_0.pdf.

Jabo, J. (2011). "Uganda must say no to homosexuality," *The Observer* 2011–05–01.

Jayawardena, K. (1986). Feminism and nationalism in the Third World. London: Zed Books.

Jeater, D. (1993). *Marriage, Perversion, and Power: The Construction of Moral Discourse in Southern Rhodesia, 1894–1930*. Oxford: Clarendon Press.

———. (2007). *Law, language, and science: the invention of the "native mind" in Southern Rhodesia, 1890–1930*. Greenwood Publishing Group.

Jjuuko, A. (2013). The incremental approach: Uganda's struggle for the decriminalization of homosexuality. Corinne Lennox and Matthew Waites (eds). *Human Rights, Sexual Orientation and Gender Identity in The Commonwealth: Struggles for Decriminalization and Change*, London: School of Advanced Study, University of London; 381–408.

Johansson, W., & Percy, W. A. (1997). Homosexuals in Nazi Germany. ed. H. Friedlander and S. Milton, Simon Wiesenthal Center Annual, 7, 225–63.

Jordan, M. D. (1997). *The Invention of Sodomy in Christian Theology*. Chicago: The University of Chicago Press.

Juris, J. S. (2007). Practicing militant ethnography with the movement for global resistance in Barcelona. *Constituent imagination: Militant investigations, collective theorization*, 164–178.

Kaoma, K. (2009). Globalizing the Culture Wars: U.S. Conservatives, African Churches, & Homophobia. *Political Research Associates*.

Karimi, F., & Thompson, N. (2014). Uganda's President Museveni signs controversial anti-gay bill into law. *CNN*, Feb. 25, 2014.

Kasasira, R. (2014). Joy, anger as Museveni signs law against gays. *The Daily Monitor*. 2015–25–2.

Katz, J. N. (1990). The invention of heterosexuality. *Race, Class and Gender, An Anthology*, 252–264.

Keating, C. (2007). Framing the Postcolonial Sexual Contract: Democracy, Fraternalism, and State Authority in India. *Hypatia*, *22*(4), 130–145.

Keck, M. and Kathryn Sikkink. 1998. *Activists Beyond Borders: Advocacy Networks in International Politics*. Ithaca: Cornell University Press.

Khapoya, V. (1994). *The African Experience: An Introduction* (1st edition ed.). Englewood Cliffs, NJ: Prentice Hall.

Kirby, M. (2011). The sodomy offence: England's least lovely criminal law export. *Journal of Commonwealth Criminal Law*, *1*, 22.

Lazarus, L. (2011). Heteronationalism, Human Rights, and the Nation-State: Positioning Sexuality in the Jamaican Constitutional Reform Process. *Canadian Journal of Latin American and Caribbean Studies*, *36*(71), 71–108.

Lister, R. (1990) Women, Economic Dependency and Citizenship, *Journal of Social Policy* 19(4): 445–68.

———. (1996) Citizenship Engendered in D. Taylor (ed.) *Critical Social Policy: A Reader*. London: Sage.

———. (1997) *Citizenship: Feminist Perspectives*. London: Macmillan.

Llewellyn, C. (2016). Homonationalism and Sexual Orientation-based Asylum Cases in the United States. *Sexualities, 20*(5–6), 682–698.

Luibheid, E. (1998). "Looking like a Lesbian": The Organization of Sexual Monitoring at the United States-Mexican Border. *Journal of the History of Sexuality*, 477–506.

———. (2002). *Entry denied: Controlling sexuality at the border*. Minneapolis: University of Minnesota Press.

Mbembé, A. (2003). Necropolitics. Translated by Meintjes, L. *Public culture*, 15(1), 11–40.

McAdam, D. (1988). *Freedom Summer*. New York: Oxford University Press.

McClelland, M. (2012). The Love that Dares. *Mother Jones*. January/Feburary 2012 Issue.

Millett, K. (1970). *Sexual politics*. New York: Doubleday.

Minor, O. (2014). Kuchus in the Balance: Queer Lives under Uganda's Anti-Homosexuality Bill (Doctoral dissertation under name *Melissa Minor Peters*, Northwestern University).

Morris, J. (2006). Gullah Island Dispute Resolution: An Example of Afrocentric Restorative Justice. *Journal of Black Studies*, (2), 299. doi:10.1177/0021934705277497.

Moya, P. M. (2002). *Learning from experience: Minority identities, multicultural struggles*. Berkeley: University of California Press.

Mugerwa R.D., M. L. H. Serwadda D. (1996). Human immunodeficiency virus and AIDS in Uganda.

Mukuthuria, M. (2006). Kiswahili and its expanding roles of development in East African cooperation: a case of Uganda. *Nordic Journal of African Studies*, *15*(2), 154–165.

Murithi, T. (2006). African Approaches to Building Peace and Social Solidarity. *ACCORD: African Centre for the Constructive Resolution of Disputes*. http://www.accord.org.za/ajcr-issues/african-approaches-to-building-peace-and-social-solidarity/.

Mwikya, K. (2014). Unnatural and Un-African: Contesting queer-phobia by Africa's political leadership. *Feminist Africa*, *19*, 98–105.

Nannyonga-Tamusuza, S. (2002). Gender, Ethnicity and Politics in Kadongo-Kamu Music of Uganda Analysing the Song Kayanda. In Palmberg, M. and Kirkegaard, A. (eds). *Playing with identities in contemporary music in Africa*. Nordic Africa Institute.

———. (2009). Female-men, male-women, and others: constructing and negotiating gender among the Baganda of Uganda. *Journal of Eastern African Studies*, 3(2), 367–380.

Ndjio, B. (2012). Post-colonial histories of sexuality: the political invention of a libidinal African straight. *Africa*, *82*(04), 609–631.

Newbury, D. (1998). Understanding genocide. *African Studies Review*, *41*(01), 73–97.

Nichols, R. (2012). Empire and the Dispositif of Queerness. *Foucault Studies*, (14), 41–60.

Nyanzi, S. (2013). Dismantling reified African culture through localized homosexualities in Uganda. *Culture, Health and Sexuality*, 15(8), 952–967.

———. (2014). Queer Pride and protest: A reading of the bodies at Uganda's first Gay Beach Pride. *Signs: A Journal of Women in Society and Culture*. 40(1), 36–40.

Oliveira, J. M. (2014). Hyphenations: The Other Lives of Feminist and Queer Concepts. *Lambda Nordica* (1).

Oyēwùmí, O. (1997). *The invention of women: Making an African sense of western gender discourses*. Minneapolis: University of Minnesota Press.

———. (2005). Colonizing Bodies and Minds. In G. G. D. A. S. Nair (Ed.), *Postcolonialisms: an anthology of cultural theory and criticism*.

Pakenham, T. (1992). *Scramble for Africa: White man's conquest of the dark continent from 1876–1912*. New York: Harper Collins.

Parikh, S. A. (2004). Sugar daddies and sexual citizenship in Uganda: rethinking third wave feminism. *Black Renaissance*, 6(1), 82.

———. (2007). The political economy of marriage and HIV: the ABC approach, "safe" infidelity, and managing moral risk in Uganda. *American journal of public health*, *97*(7), 1198.

Parkhurst, J. O. (2002). The Ugandan success story? Evidence and claims of HIV-1 prevention. *The Lancet*, *360*(9326), 78–80.

Pateman, C. (1988). *The sexual contract*. Stanford: Stanford University Press.

———. (1989). *The disorder of women: Democracy, feminism and political theory*. Stanford: Stanford University Press.

Petras, J. F., & Veltmeyer, H. (2001). *Globalization unmasked: Imperialism in the 21st century*. London: Zed Books.

Pew Research Center. (2013). A Survey of LGBT Americans. Accessed via: http://www.pewsocialtrends.org/2013/06/13/a-survey-of-lgbt-americans/.

Plant, R. (1986). *The pink triangle. The nazi war against homosexuals*. New York: Henry Holt and Company.

Puar, J. K. (1998). Transnational sexualities: South Asian (trans)nation(alism)s and queer diasporas. *Q&A: Queer in Asian America*, 405–422.

———. (2007). *Terrorist assemblages: Homonationalism in queer times*. Durham: Duke University Press.

Rao, R. (2015). Re-membering Mwanga: same-sex intimacy, memory and belonging in postcolonial Uganda. *Journal of Eastern African Studies*, *9*(1), 1–19.

Reisner, S. L., Bailey, Z., & Sevelius, J. (2014). Racial/ethnic disparities in history of incarceration, experiences of victimization, and associated health indicators among transgender women in the US. *Women & health*, 54(8), 750–767.

Richardson, D. (1998). Sexuality and citizenship. *Sociology*, *32*(1), 83–100.

———. (2000). Constructing sexual citizenship: theorizing sexual rights. *Critical Social Policy*.

Richardson, E. H., & Turner, B. S. (2001). Sexual, intimate or reproductive citizenship? *Citizenship studies*, *5*(3), 329–338.

Ring, T. (2018). These Are the Trans People Killed in 2018. *The Advocate*. Accessed 26 July 2018: https://www.advocate.com/transgender/2018/6/04/these-are-trans-people-killed-2018#media-gallery-media-0.

Rodriguez, SM. (2017). Homophobic Nationalism: The development of anti-sodomy legislation in Uganda. *Comparative Sociology*, 16(3).

Robson, R., & Kessler, T. (2008). Unsettling sexual citizenship. *McGill LJ*, *53*, 535–807.

Roy, A. (2014). The NGO-ization of Resistance. Toward Freedom, Accessed at: queensneighborhoodsunited.org

Russell, T. (2008). The color of discipline: Civil rights and black sexuality. *American Quarterly*, 60(1), 101–128.

Sadgrove, J., Vanderbeck, R.M., Andersson, J., Valentine, G., and Ward, K. (2012). Morality plays and money matters: towards a situated understanding of the politics of homosexuality in Uganda. . *The Journal of Modern African Studies, 50*, pp 103–129.

Sandoval, C. (1991). US third world feminism: The theory and method of oppositional consciousness in the postmodern world. *Genders*, (10), 1–24.

———. (2000). *Methodology of the Oppressed* (Vol. 18). Minneapolis: University of Minnesota Press.

Saukko, P. (2003). *Doing research in cultural studies: An introduction to classical and new methodological approaches* (Vol. 137). Sage.

Schilt, K. (2006). Just one of the guys? How transmen make gender visible at work. *Gender & Society*, 20(4), 465–490.

Schlanger, Z. (2014). "American Quakers are Running New Underground Railroad to Help LGBT Ugandans Flee." *Newsweek*.

Seidman, S. (2001). From identity to queer politics: Shifts in normative heterosexuality and the meaning of citizenship. *Citizenship Studies*, *5*(3), 321–328.

Senteza, C. (2003). Lesbian and Gay Identity in Uganda: A Christian Vision for my Country. *Address for Lesbian and Gay Christian Movement (LGCM) Conference*. Accessed through archive: chttps://web.archive.org/web/20080512092907/http://www.lgcm.org.uk/HalfwayToLambeth/Speeches/Sentenza.htm.

Sircar, O., & Jain, D. (2012). Editor's Introduction: New Intimacies/Old Desires: Law, Culture and Queer Politics in Neoliberal Times. *Jindal Global L. Rev.*, 4, 1–16.

Smith, A. (2001). Introduction. Incite! Women of Color Against Violence. The Revolution Will Not Be Funded: Beyond the Non-Profit Industrial Complex.

Smith, J. (1997). Characteristics of the modern transnational social movement sector. Transnational social movements and global politics: Solidarity beyond the state, 42–58.

Smith, J. G., Smith, J., & Johnston, H. (Eds.). (2002). *Globalization and resistance: Transnational Dimensions of Social Movements*. Rowman & Littlefield.

Smith, J. and Wiest, D. (2005). The Uneven Geography of Global Civil Society: National and Global Influences on Transnational Association. The University of North Carolina Press. *Social Forces*, 84(2).

SMUG. (2005). Uganda Human Rights Commission Receives an Official Petition from SMUG.

———. (2007). UGANDAN HOMOSEXUALS Close Media Campaign: "LET US LIVE IN PEACE" https://www.outrightinternational.org/content/uganda-sexual-minorities-uganda-smug-close-media-campaign.

———. (2014a). Expanded Criminalisation of Homosexuality in Uganda: A Flawed Narrative. (retrieved from www.sexualminoritiesuganda.com).

———. (2014b). From Torment to Tyranny: Enhanced Persecution in Uganda Following the Passage of the Anti-Homosexuality Act 2014.

Solórzano, D. G., & Yosso, T. J. (2002). Critical race methodology: Counter-storytelling as an analytical framework for education research. *Qualitative inquiry*, 8(1), 23–44.

Somerville, S. B. (2005). Notes toward a queer history of naturalization. *American quarterly, 57*(3), 659–675.

Stoler, A. L. (1995). *Race and the education of desire: Foucault's History of sexuality and the Colonial Order of Things*. Durham: Duke University Press Books.

———. (1997). Making Empire Respectable; The Politics of Race and Sexual Morality in Twentieth-Century Colonial Cultures. *Cultural Politics, 11*, 344–373.

———. (2002). *Carnal knowledge and imperial power: race and the intimate in colonial rule*. Berkeley: University of California Press.

Tamale, S. (2008). The right to culture and the culture of rights: A critical perspective on women's sexual rights in Africa. *Feminist Legal Studies*, 16(1), 47–69.

———. (2009). A human rights impact assessment of the Ugandan Anti-homosexuality Bill 2009. *Equal Rights Review, 4*(49–57).

Taylor and Nella Van Dyke. (2004). "'Get Up, Stand Up': Tactical Repertoires of Social Movements." Pp. 262–293 in *The Blackwell Companion to Social Movements*, edited by David A. Snow, Sarah A. Soule, and Hanspeter Kriesi. Malden, MA: Blackwell.

Thoreson, R. R. (2014a). *Transnational LGBT activism: Working for sexual rights worldwide*. Minneapolis: University of Minnesota Press.

———. (2014b). Troubling the waters of a 'wave of homophobia': Political economies of anti-queer animus in sub-Saharan Africa. *Sexualities*. 17(1/2) 23–42.

Timberg, C. (2007). Uganda's Early Gains Against HIV Eroding, *The Washington Post*. Retrieved from http://www.washingtonpost.com/wp-dyn/content/article/2007/03/28/AR2007032802510.html.

Tripp, A. M. (2001). The new political activism in Africa. *Journal of democracy*, 12(3), 141–155.

——— (2001). The politics of autonomy and cooptation in Africa: The case of the Ugandan Women's Movement. The Journal of Modern African Studies, 39(1), 101–128. doi:10.1017/S0022278X01003548.

———. (2004). Women's movements, customary law, and land rights in Africa: the case of Uganda. *African Studies Quarterly*, 7(4), 1–19.

Tuhiwai Smith, L. (1999). Decolonizing methodologies: Research and indigenous peoples. London: Zed Books, 2ed.

Turner, B. S. (2008). *The body and society: Explorations in social theory*. Sage.

Tutu, D. (1999). *No future without Forgiveness*. Image Books.

Twine, F.W., Warren, J.W. (Eds.). (2000). *Racing research, researching race: Methodological dilemmas in critical race studies*. New York: NYU Press.

Uganda Penal Code Act World Intellectual Property Organization. (1950).

Ungar, M. (2000). State Violence and Lesbian, Gay, Bisexual, and Transgender (lgbt) Rights. *New Political Science* 22(1): 61–75.

Wahab, A. (2016). Calling 'Homophobia'into Place (Jamaica) Homo/trans/nationalism in the Stop Murder Music (Canada) Campaign. *Interventions*, 18(6), 908–928.

Wallerstein, I. (1974a). The Rise and Future Demise of the of the World-Capitalist System: Concepts for Comparative Analysis. *Comparative Studies in Society and History* 16: 387–415.

———. (1974b). *The Modern World-System: Capitalist Agriculture and the Origins of the European World-Economy in the Sixteenth Century*. New York: Academic Press.

Wapner, P. (1996). *Environmental Activism and World Civic Politics*. New York: City University of New York Press.

Ward, K. (2013). Religious Institutions and Actors and Religious Attitudes to Homosexual Rights: South Africa and Uganda. in C Lennox & M Waites (eds.), *Human Rights, Sexual Orientation and Gender Identity in the Commonwealth: Struggles for Decriminalisation and Change*. Institute of Commonwealth Studies.

Warkentin, C. and Mingst, K. (2000). International Institutions, the State, and Global Civil Society in the Age of the World Wide Web. *Global Governance* 6:237–257.

Weeks, J. (1981). Sex, Politics and Society: The Regulation of Sexuality Since 1900. 48–52.

White, M. A. (2013). Ambivalent homonationalisms: transnational queer intimacies and territorialized belongings. *Interventions*, *15*(1), 37–54.

Index

About the Author

S.M. Rodriguez is a scholar-activist and assistant professor of sociology and criminology at Hofstra University, in New York. A community organizer dedicated to gender, sexual, and racial justice, they have coordinated dozens of workshops and events on community safety from policing and gentrification in central Brooklyn. They also provide security for protests by LGBTQ people of color throughout NYC. Dr. Rodriguez's research interests span Black and queer empowerment and self-determination. Their newest bodies of work focus on the militarization of the police and mass incarceration in the United States. They are currently working on a book on queer abolitionist organizing in Brooklyn, New York.

www.ingramcontent.com/pod-product-compliance
Lightning Source LLC
Chambersburg PA
CBHW050614280326
41932CB00016B/3038

* 9 7 8 1 4 9 8 5 8 1 7 3 8 *